GLOW POPS

GLOW
POPS

SUPER-EASY SUPERFOOD RECIPES
TO HELP YOU LOOK AND FEEL YOUR BEST

LIZ MOODY

PHOTOGRAPHY BY LAUREN VOLO

CLARKSON POTTER/PUBLISHERS
New York

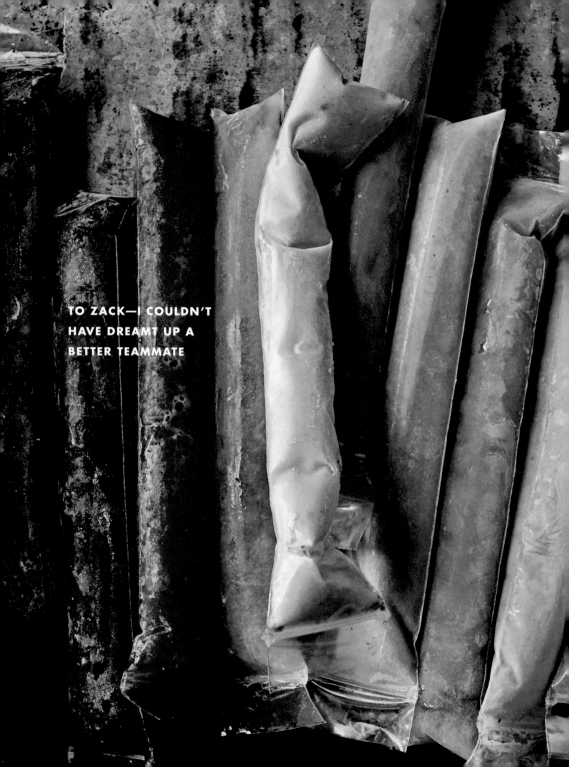

TO ZACK—I COULDN'T
HAVE DREAMT UP A
BETTER TEAMMATE

CONTENTS

INTRODUCTION

I've always been a firm believer that having a healthy life doesn't have to be limiting or difficult. Every time a new health trend sweeps the country—whether it's expensive pressed juices or imported Asian jungle fruits or powdered superfoods with exotic names—I find myself equally excited and frustrated. Excited because I *love* that the health conversation has become mainstream! No longer relegated to the subcultures, the desire to eat well and nourish our bodies has become common. Natural supermarkets are popping up all over the country, sales at McDonald's are at an all-time low, and people are finally asking, "What are all these man-made ingredients I can't pronounce doing in my food? Is this something I should be putting in my body?"

I'm frustrated, though, because the health world can feel exclusive and intimidating. My health philosophy relies on a simple rule: eat whole, real foods. That's it! You don't need a dehydrator or hours and hours of free time or a local farmers' market that's filled with heirloom apples and microgreens (although if you have any of those things, that's wonderful too!). All you need is a desire to nourish your body and an appetite for the delicious bounty that comes from our earth.

This is one of the many reasons I'm such a fan of Glow Pops, healthy, nourishing pops that fill you with energy and nutrients and make you absolutely glow. Once you nail a few simple tricks to ensure you get the right texture every time, you can have a ton of fun playing around with different flavor profiles. A Glow Pop is the opposite of a boring, flavorless salad—and it often has far more in the way of nutrients. Anything that gets people not only eating nutritious food but truly enjoying it—well, that's a real win.

I didn't always view food like this. When I was in college, I was obsessed with calorie counting, giving far more credence to the numbers on the back of my packaged foods than what was actually *in* them. I was perpetually hungry,

plagued with skin problems, and couldn't get rid of the excess fat I had around my belly, no matter how few calories I ate.

At the time, I was working as a newspaper columnist. For my column, I'd often find myself traveling around the world, going on adventures that I could share with my audience. Along the way, I began to notice how local cultures viewed food. Most approached both making and eating it with much more joy than I did. Instead of nuking a two-minute meal, people were soaking grains overnight, letting a tagine simmer for hours, and spending entire evenings at the table, laughing and chatting and sipping wine well after the food was finished. In many of these cultures, the people were also healthier than most of the population back home: strong and slender, with clear skin and long, healthy hair.

Intrigued, I dove deeper into the gastronomical world. I took cooking classes in Italy and Syria, and a short sommelier course in Paris. I even worked on a farm in the South of France, plowing fields and turning goat's milk into creamy, tangy cheese. At the same time, I began to note all the ways food was used as medicine.

When I returned to the United States, my approach to food had completely changed—and so had my body. My skin had cleared up and my body had effortlessly found its happy weight (absolutely no calorie counting required!). I felt vibrant and full of energy, excited about the possibilities food held, for both my taste buds and my health, like never before.

I started my blog, Sprouted Routes, as a way to share this knowledge and all the easy, healthy, delectable recipes I've developed in the years since. Sprouted Routes is all about easy paths to a healthy, beautiful life. Health doesn't have to be difficult. It doesn't have to be bland or ugly or more "crunchy" or less delicious. It can be glamorous, gorgeous, and bursting with flavor and life. And it can be fun, which is where Glow Pops come in!

I've infused many of these recipes with the flavor profiles and ancient, natural remedies I picked up on my international adventures. Every pop in this book is made with whole, nutritious foods and is gluten-free, dairy-free, refined-sugar-free, and optionally vegan. There are pops for weight loss, pops to decrease your bloat, and pops to make your skin glow. There are antiviral, antifungal, and antibacterial pops as well as antioxidant-packed pops. There are pops designed to soothe specific conditions—when my summer allergies kick in, I make a batch of Turmeric Golden Milk pops weekly to keep the itchy eyes and sniffles at bay. If I know I'm going to be spending a lot of time outside, I rely on Cucumber Mint Mojito pops, which contain ingredients that help protect against skin cancer. And, of course, I keep a stash of Tomato Beet Bloody Mary pops in the freezer at all times—there's no better (or better tasting!) way to quickly get rid of a hangover.

While I love to eat pops as a healthy way to satisfy my sweet tooth in lieu of traditional desserts, many of the pops contain enough fiber, good fat, and protein to make incredibly healthy meals. Because you make pops in batches and then simply grab them, fully finished, from the freezer, they're ready in less time than it takes to whip up a smoothie or toast an English muffin. During the summer, my husband grabs a Peanut Butter & Jelly pop on his way to work most mornings.

And by the way—pops are simply fun! While adults love Glow Pops, often kids love them even more, and they're a great way to sneak more healthy foods into even the pickiest eater's diet. Because most of the recipes are quite easy to prepare, it's fun to bring kids into the kitchen from the beginning, letting them be involved in the actual preparation of the pops. My four-year-old niece is obsessed with the Cardamom Cinnamon Sweet Potato pop, while my girlfriend's seven-year-old son, who turns his nose up at all vegetables, is obsessed with the spinach-packed Mint Chocolate Chip green smoothie pop.

If you want to up the ante on the health benefits of your pops even more, be sure to check out the superfoods section (page 19), where I tell you how to sneak in ingredients like vitamin C–rich camu camu, protein-packed hemp seeds, hormone-balancing maca, and many more. These pops are a great option if you have specific needs you're trying to address or simply want to take it to the next level!

So if you're already health conscious, I applaud you, and invite you to treat yourself to a Glow Pop. And if you're not—well, you've picked a great way to start your journey, and I'm so proud to be part of its beginning!

GETTING STARTED

Glow Pops are super simple to make, but there are a few things that will ensure you have perfect pops every single time. In this section, we'll discuss the few pieces of equipment you'll need, some notes on ingredients to make sure you're getting all the glow-inducing health benefits, and information on how to unmold and store your pops. Are you ready? Let's get glowing!

EQUIPMENT

Pops are one of the easiest things you can make in your kitchen, but there are still a few key pieces of equipment you need, from the molds you'll freeze your pops in to the blender that turns fresh, beautiful ingredients into a sweet, smooth pop mixture! Luckily, there's quite a bit of flexibility in both, and you'll likely find you have much of what you need in your kitchen already.

MOLDS

All pops begin with molds, also known as the things that give them their shape and make them, well, pops! There are plenty of different brands available on the market, and they come in shapes from swirls and stars to fish and rocket ships. You don't need to spend much to get a great one.

Two of my favorites, from Zoku and Norpro, are available for under $20 in home goods stores, big box retailers, specialty kitchen goods shops, and online. The Zoku Classic Pop Molds come with built-in, reusable plastic sticks that have drip guards, while the Norpro Ice Pop Maker utilizes wooden sticks and has the classic shape you might remember from childhood, with lines down the side. There are also silicone molds that make push-up pops, and some newer, quick-freezing models out there, for those of you who are impatient (I'm raising my hand!), although they cost a bit more. (Because of the fast freezing time, they'll also result in a slightly creamier pop texture.) You can get great results with almost any mold. I've made pops in over twenty different types of molds, and the results were almost identical across the board, so it really comes down to your preference. My one caveat: Always look for a mold that is BPA-free, which will almost always be touted on the box or in the description.

Because they're relatively inexpensive, I do recommend buying a mold if you're planning on making pops regularly. There are, however, a few good alternatives. Small paper or plastic cups (like the kind typically found in the bathroom or the dentist's office) make cute, fun size pops, and plastic Champagne flutes make a surprisingly classic shape (just leave room at the top for the liquid to expand, and be careful when placing them in the freezer). Ice cube trays will make bite-size pops, which are fun for parties or kids. While most molds do come with sticks, if you're DIY-ing it, you can buy wooden sticks at most craft stores or online.

Note that the recipes in this book are all designed to make five or six 3-ounce pops, which is the standard size of most molds. If you're using a DIY mold, the recipes will likely yield a slightly different amount. If you have any extra unfrozen mixture left over, you can either drink it (sometimes I can't help but sneak sips anyway!) or store it in an airtight container in the fridge until the first batch of pops is frozen, and then use it to make a second batch.

BLENDER

My blender is one of my kitchen workhorses. If you can, I recommend investing in a high-power blender: it will give you creamier, smoother results, especially with things that can be a bit harder to blend, like dates or greens. I splurged on a Vitamix a few years ago, and my only regret is not doing it sooner. I use it every single day and love using it to make Glow Pops. If you're not quite there yet, no worries! There are wonderful blenders at every price point—both the NutriBullet Pro 900 and the Waring Pro PBB225 make wonderful pops and clock in at under $100. If you're using a less powerful blender, just let it run a little longer than recommended in the recipe, then turn off the blender and sneak in a spoon for a taste. If it's not quite smooth enough for you, give it an extra 30 seconds or a minute!

FOOD PROCESSOR

For the Fruity pops (page 27), it also helps to have a food processor, although it's not completely necessary. Because fruits are so juicy, we're adding little to no additional liquid, and food processors are more adept at making all-fruit purees. You can find great food processors between $100 and $200 at kitchen stores and online. I personally love the 6-, 8-, and 11-cup KitchenAid and Cuisinart models, but really any type will work fine. You don't need anything fancy in a food processor—I strongly recommend ignoring all the crazy new features and getting a simple machine that's built to last. If you don't have a food processor, don't worry—where I suggest using one, just add water 1 tablespoon at a time until your blender whizzes the fruit right up.

INGREDIENTS

While the basic form of pops is always the same—you mix or blend ingredients, then freeze them—one of my favorite things about them is their flexibility. They're nowhere near as finicky as traditional baked desserts, which require exact chemical reactions and a precise order to their process. Pops are almost impossible to truly mess up, and you can taste them as you go along and adjust accordingly. Feel free to use this book as a rough guide, and play around with the recipes to make them suit you! Let's go over some basic ingredients you'll see again and again.

SWEETENERS

The recipes here use five different sweeteners: maple syrup, coconut sugar, coconut syrup, honey, and dates. Unlike white or cane sugar, these are all still in their whole food form, and therefore haven't been stripped of their nutrients. They all have different advantages and nutritional properties. Maple syrup, coconut syrup, and honey are liquid and thus easy to dissolve at room

UNMOLDING AND STORING YOUR POPS

To unmold your pops, simply run the molds under warm water for about 10 seconds, then pull the sticks to remove the pops. You can eat them immediately or, if you want to save them for later, lay them flat on a piece of parchment paper on a baking sheet or plate. Place in the freezer for 1 hour after unmolding, or until completely frozen again; after that, you can transfer to a plastic zip-top bag and store for up to 3 months. If you're using small paper cups to make your pops, simply store in the freezer until you're ready to eat, then peel off the paper and devour!

temperature, for instance, while coconut syrup and coconut sugar have some of the lowest glycemic index numbers of any sweetener, making them a great choice for diabetics or others with blood sugar issues. Dates are a whole fruit and still contain all of their fiber, but may not blend as well in the smoother pops, so I prefer to use them only in green smoothie pops.

For each recipe, I've selected the sweetener I think works best for the pop, in terms of both texture and flavor. If you prefer something different, go ahead and substitute it! Maple syrup, coconut sugar, coconut syrup, and honey can all be substituted for each other in a 1:1 ratio, and each tablespoon of maple syrup, coconut sugar, coconut syrup, and honey is equal to 1 date. If you choose to use dates, you'll typically have the best results with the Medjool variety, which tend to be softer and more caramel-like in texture, and are, as a result, easier to blend with the rest of your ingredients (see page 21). If you're using another type of date, be sure to soak them in boiling water for 10 to 20 minutes to soften them quite a bit and make them far more blendable; drain them well before using.

All these can be purchased online and at most grocery stores and health food stores. Coconut syrup is a bit rarer than coconut sugar, but it's super easy to make at home. Here's how:

COCONUT SYRUP

MAKES ½ CUP

- 1 cup coconut sugar
- ½ cup water

In a small saucepan, whisk together the coconut sugar and water, then bring to a boil over medium-high heat. Reduce the heat to medium-low and simmer, uncovered, for 20 minutes, or until thick and syrupy—no need to stir. Remove the pan from the heat and let the syrup cool completely before using. Store in an airtight container in the fridge for up to 2 weeks.

For optimal nutrition, I recommend buying raw honey, as it still contains all its enzymes and nutrients. As an added bonus, if you buy local raw honey, it'll act as a mild inoculant against allergies prevalent in your area!

If you're having a hard time finding reasonably priced Medjool dates, I recommend checking out Middle Eastern markets (a great place to buy affordable spices as well!).

Flavor preferences are individual, and what I consider perfectly sweet might be too sweet or not sweet enough for you, so be sure to taste your pop mix before pouring it into the molds, and adjust the sweetener as needed. Remember that the cold dulls our perception of sweetness, so you want your unfrozen pop mixture to taste just a little bit sweeter than how you want the final pops to taste.

MILKS

I prefer to use nondairy milks to make pops, for reasons of both health and texture. The trick to a good creamy pop is having milk that's less watery than typical dairy milk. Canned coconut milk, available at almost any grocery store, works beautifully in pops—it's thick enough to give a super-creamy, hearty texture. Coconut milk is definitely my favorite kind to use in any of these recipes. I've had good results with both light and full-fat. The latter is slightly creamier, but both will give great results. If you're wondering if all your pops will taste like coconut, the answer is no! The flavor of coconut milk actually is interpreted by our tongues as sweetness, so if anything, that's all it will add in flavor.

When cold, canned coconut milk will separate into a thick white top layer (sometimes called coconut cream) and a watery bottom layer. This is completely normal, so don't panic! To make the texture homogenous again, simply toss both layers into a blender and whiz for a few seconds, or heat it gently over low heat on the stove, stirring occasionally, then use as the recipe directs. It's always a good idea to shake the can before opening it, too.

As for almond, rice, hemp, and soy milks, the types that now fill supermarket aisles have too thin a consistency to make a great pop. You can use them if you

COCONUT MILK

MAKES 2 CUPS

- 1¼ cups water
- 1 cup dried unsweetened flaked coconut

In a small pot, bring the water to a boil. Put the coconut in a bowl and pour the boiling water over it. Set aside to soak for 30 minutes. Transfer the mixture to a blender and blend on high for 2 to 3 minutes, or until very smooth. Strain through a nut milk bag, or pour into a clean dishtowel set over a clean container. "Milk" the bag or towel until all the liquid has passed through; discard the remaining pulp or reserve for another use. Store in an airtight container in the fridge for up to 5 days.

ALMOND MILK

MAKES 2 CUPS

- 1 cup almonds
- 1¼ cups water

Soak the almonds in filtered water to cover for 12 to 24 hours, then drain. In a blender, blend the soaked almonds and water on high for 2 to 3 minutes or until very smooth. Strain through a nut milk bag, or pour into a clean dishtowel set over a clean container. "Milk" the bag or towel until all the liquid has passed through; discard the remaining pulp or reserve for another use. Store in an airtight container in the fridge for up to 5 days.

CASHEW MILK

MAKES 2 CUPS

- 1 cup cashews
- 1¼ cups water

Soak the cashews in filtered water for 4 to 6 hours, then drain. In a blender, blend the soaked cashews and water on high for 2 to 3 minutes, or until very smooth. No need to strain. Store in an airtight container in the fridge for up to 5 days.

like, but you might end up with an icier pop. There are a few ways to combat this, so be sure to check out A Note About Texture on page 23.

Homemade milks are incredibly easy to make—the process basically involves soaking, blending, and straining. I often will make a big batch on Sunday or Monday and leave it my fridge for smoothies, pops, and other recipes (curry, pancakes, cereal) throughout the week. See page 17 for the recipes. But if a recipe calls for another type of milk—let's say, almond—and you don't feel like making your own, you can *always* substitute canned coconut milk in a 1:1 ratio.

FRUIT

I specify in each recipe whether to use fresh or frozen fruit. In general, for the "fruity" pops, which rely on fruit as the superstar for texture and flavor, you'll want to buy fresh, while the rest of the pops will do fine with frozen. For the green smoothie pops in particular, I tend to use frozen berries, as they're cheaper and easier to find than fresh and you don't have to worry about their spoiling. Frozen berries are often healthier than fresh as well, as nutrients like vitamin C decline rapidly from the moment a berry is picked. Because frozen berries are flash-frozen just after they've been picked at peak ripeness, all that goodness is locked in, ready and waiting to be delivered to your body.

In general, for any fruit where you're using the skin, it's best to buy organic. For fruits like avocado and banana, conventional is fine; when in doubt, consult the Environmental Working Group's Dirty Dozen list for the most heavily sprayed produce. While conventional citrus is typically fine, many Glow Pop recipes call for the fruit to be zested, as citrus zest is packed with highly nutritious oils that are amazing for your skin. When using citrus skin, I strongly recommend buying organic. For any produce where you'll be eating the skin but can't find organic, soak the fruit in a 1:1 mix of apple cider vinegar and water for 10 minutes, then wash and dry well to remove any (not glow-worthy!) pesticide residue.

SUPERFOOD ADD-INS

The following are my go-to superfoods to ramp up the health factor of the pops even more. I want to stress that you don't *need* these in any of the pops—even without them, all the Glow Pops are bursting with health benefits. That said, if you have specific health issues you're trying to address or simply want to take your pop to the next level, these add-ins are great. To use, simply add the superfood when you add whatever liquid you're using in the pop and blend until smooth. The quantities listed are appropriate for five or six 3-ounce pops.

2 tablespoons hulled hemp seeds—Hemp seeds offer one of the only forms of complete protein in the natural world. One tablespoon contains 5.3 grams protein, plus 13 percent of your daily iron and 8 percent of your daily vitamin A. Hemp adds a subtle nutty flavor and wonderful creaminess. Blend the hemp seeds with whatever liquid you're using, then proceed with the rest of the recipe as instructed. This would work well in any pops.

1 tablespoon lucuma powder—Lucuma powder is made from the South American lucuma fruit, which is dried at a low temperature and then ground into a powder. It's rich in vitamin A, which is fundamental for glowing skin, and vitamin B3, or niacin, which is mostly found in meat sources and in which many vegetarians are deficient. It has a lightly sweet, caramel flavor that's delicious in any pops that use maple syrup, coconut sugar, or dates as a sweetener.

1 tablespoon maca powder—This superfood is made from a South American root plant that is dried at low temperatures and then milled into a fine powder. It is noted for its hormone-balancing capabilities, and can be a great supplement for people dealing with low sex drive, menstrual cycle irregularities, hormonal skin conditions, and similar problems. It's also adaptogenic, which means that it adapts to the individualized needs of your body—you will respond differently to it than your friends and family might. It tends to make people feel more energized, but not in the buzzy way that's associated with caffeine. Outside of its adaptogenic properties, maca is rich in protein, vitamins, and minerals. It adds a malty quality to whatever you blend it into. I like it best in the Cookie Dough, Chocolate Fudge, and Chocolate Caramel Swirl pops and the Double Chocolate Brownie green smoothie pop. Because maca is a powerful herb, it can be best to start with a smaller amount (1 teaspoon per recipe) before working your way up to the full tablespoon.

1 tablespoon açai powder—Açai (pronounced *ah-SIGH-ee)* is an Amazonian fruit that is freeze-dried and ground into powder. It has risen in popularity in recent years due to its incredibly high antioxidant content and its uniquely creamy texture from the high level of essential fatty acids. It has a sweet flavor not unlike that of blackberries and blueberries, and works well in any of the berry-based pops.

1 tablespoon camu camu powder—Camu camu is a fruit grown throughout the Amazon rain forest. Its claim to fame is its vitamin C content: it has more than any other food source on the planet! This is a great addition if you want to naturally boost your immune system. The powder has a tart berry flavor and works well in any of the berry-based pops or in pops with a slightly tart flavor, like Pink Lemonade or Lemon Ginger.

1 tablespoon whole flaxseeds—Fiber-rich flaxseeds are the richest source of plant-based omega-3s in the world, making them anti-inflammatory superstars. They're also rich in lignans—phytonutrients that help regulate hormone levels, which positively affects stress levels and hormonal conditions like PMS, and may even help prevent certain types of cancer. The problem with flaxseeds is that they easily go rancid, losing their health benefits and developing an unappetizing flavor when exposed to light and air. This is even more true after they're ground—but they need to be ground well in order to be absorbed by our bodies, rather than simply passing through. This is why I love incorporating them in green smoothie pops—they're ground by the blender and then immediately frozen, which prevents oxidation and allows their awesome nutritional properties to stay intact. Flaxseeds have a very subtle nutty flavor, and work well in all the green smoothie pops. Store your flaxseeds in an opaque container in the freezer to preserve their freshness.

SPECIAL INGREDIENTS

There are a handful of ingredients included in these recipes that you may not have in your pantry already. They're not super hard to find, but they come up a bunch, so let's take a look before you dive in and get your glow on.

Medjool dates—Creamier and more caramel-y than Deglet Noors, Medjool dates are worth hunting down. I've found them at many natural food stores, at Whole Foods, and at Middle Eastern markets, where they are often sold in bulk at amazing prices. You can also find them online, usually for about $10 a pound. Just remember to remove the pit when using Medjool dates—they always come fully intact!

Culinary lavender—When a recipe calls for lavender, you want to be sure to buy the culinary variety, as the type you find in sachets or some gardens is sprayed with chemicals that aren't meant to be ingested. You can find culinary lavender at higher-end food and baking supply shops, like Williams-Sonoma and Dean & DeLuca; in the spice section at some higher-end supermarkets (Whole Foods usually has it); and, my personal favorite, online (just be sure to search for "food-grade" or "culinary" lavender).

Rose water—Rose water can be found at many Middle Eastern or Indian markets, usually for less than $5 a bottle. Because it's a common ingredient in many cocktail recipes, you'll also have good luck at higher-end liquor stores. It's also widely available online.

Matcha—A powdered green tea, matcha has become hugely popular in recent years and is now available in most grocery stores and online. Matcha comes in two types: culinary grade and the more expensive ceremonial grade. For pops, culinary grade will work just fine, although if you already have the more finely milled ceremonial grade on hand, that will work beautifully as well!

Salt—Salt isn't rare, but it's worth mentioning here. While any type of salt will work fine in these pops, I highly recommend using sea salt or pink Himalayan salt, which hasn't undergone the same bleaching and processing as typical white table salt, and has a much lower sodium and higher mineral content as a result. I also find unprocessed salt to be faintly sweet in a way that truly elevates a pop's flavor. You can find mineral-rich salt online or at most grocery stores for a very reasonable price.

Cacao—All the chocolate pops derive their flavor from some type of raw cacao, whether it be in the form of powder, nibs, or butter. Cacao nibs are made from breaking the cacao bean into small pieces and are the least processed form of cacao. Cacao powder is made from grinding nibs into a fine powder, usually using a low-heat or heatless process. Both cacao nibs and cacao powder retain the maximum health benefits of the cacao bean, which include minerals like potassium, magnesium, and chromium, and an incredibly high level of antioxidants. Raw cacao also contains a unique compound called theobromine, which raises energy and alertness levels without the buzzy effect of caffeine.

Cacao butter is the pressed oil of the cacao bean. To extract the cacao butter, the nibs are pressed to separate the oil from the fiber. Like cacao, cacao butter is rich in antioxidants and theobromine, as well as oleic acid, which has been shown to reduce the risk of heart disease.

Cocoa powder and cocoa butter are essentially the same as raw cacao and raw cacao butter, except that they've been processed at high temperatures that eliminate many of cacao's health benefits. In all recipes that call for cacao powder and cacao butter, you can sub in cocoa powder and cocoa butter in a 1:1 ratio; just try to get the highest-quality you can find, to retain the most nutrients.

Cacao nibs are used for texture in addition to their flavor, and can be replaced at a 1:1 ratio with mini dark chocolate chips or coarsely chopped dark chocolate.

A NOTE ABOUT TEXTURE

There are three things that account for a pop avoiding a rock-hard texture: fat, fiber, and sugar. Traditional pops typically rely on sugar—especially simple syrup. Without getting too scientific, simple syrup wedges itself between the water molecules of the pop, so they don't bond to one another hard and tight, whereas water molecules without sugar in between them are simply ice cubes—which you definitely wouldn't want to bite into! Glow Pops never use simple sugars, so we have to get creative to achieve that perfect pop texture, relying instead on fiber and fat.

FIBER

You'll find that many other pop recipes (typically the fruity ones) call for you to strain your mixture through a fine-mesh strainer to avoid any errant texture in the pops: persistent seeds, or bits of pulp that don't quite blend up. Generally speaking, though, for both health and texture reasons I prefer not to strain Glow Pops. Straining removes quite a bit of the fruit or vegetable's fiber, which is one of the things that will prevent your pops from having an icy consistency. Leaving in the bulk from the fruit or vegetable membrane gives the batter a weight that prevents iciness. Fiber is also a wonderfully healthy ingredient, glow-worthy all on its own. It helps slow down the rate at which you digest your food, which ensures you'll stay fuller longer and avoid the nasty blood-sugar roller coaster that comes from eating sugary, fiberless foods. It also acts like a gentle scrub brush on your intestinal tract, helping move along waste and ensuring you have productive bathroom visits (a vital part of getting that glow, as accumulated waste is bloating and inflammatory in the body).

FAT

Fat is a great way to get that satisfying, creamy texture. While you might shy away from fat for fear of your health or an expanding waistline, I implore you to reconsider. Researchers are finding more and more that a number of fats are not only not bad for you, but actually have amazing health benefits.

THE FIBER-FAT DOUBLE WHAMMY: CHIA SEEDS

I use chia seeds in a number of pop recipes for their consistency: once blended, they can make a pop super creamy and wonderful to bite into. They're rich in omega-3s, and one serving contains more than 30 percent of your daily requirement for manganese, magnesium, and phosphorous. They're packed with protein and are made of almost 40 percent fiber, which makes them one of the most fiber-rich foods in the world. This fact, combined with the gelatinous coating that forms on each seed when submerged in liquid, makes them incredibly soothing to the digestive system. I love to use these if I am recovering from any sort of stomach bug or have been traveling, when my digestion is often quite backed up. Chia seeds are one of my favorite ways to achieve a creamy texture in my pops without relying on higher-fat milks. Because they're so satiating, I'll also add them to any pop I'm looking to turn into a meal replacement. They have almost no flavor and work well in any of the pops in this book.

To use, stir in 3 tablespoons chia seeds for every 1 cup of the pop mixture. You can then blend again or process in a food processor (for thicker mixtures) for optimal smoothness, or simply freeze with the chia seeds intact for a pop with bits of crunch in each bite. You may need to add a bit more liquid to get the pop to blend—do so 1 tablespoon at a time, if necessary.

Glow Pops rely only on fats that are 100 percent nourishing for your body. Full-fat coconut milk, as discussed, is my go-to base. While many people avoid full-fat products, the type of fat found in coconut is mostly in the form of medium-chain fatty acids (MCFAs) and, in particular, one called lauric acid. Unlike saturated fats found in animal products, MCFAs are almost immediately converted into energy by the body, and are unlikely to be stored as fat. Lauric acid is also considered one of nature's most potent superfoods (outside of coconut, breast milk is one of the few places it's found in nature, which proves its importance in human health and development), and is renowned for its antiviral, antibacterial, and antifungal properties.

The majority of fat in both almonds and cashews is monounsaturated fat, similar to the type found in olive oil. Monounsaturated fat is known for its heart-healthy properties, and is often recommended as a dietary inclusion for people with heart disease and diabetes. A recent study found that people who eat nuts at least twice a week are much *less* likely to gain weight than those who almost never eat nuts, so bring on the nut milks and nut butters!

The final fat I rely on is avocado, one of my favorite fruits (that's right—it's a fruit!). The majority of fat in avocados comes from oleic acid, a monounsaturated fat that reduces inflammation (the root of many chronic diseases) in the body, and has been linked with activating genes thought to be responsible for fighting many cancers, making them essentially anticarcinogenic. Avocados have a creamy, decadent texture and a mild flavor that works well as a subtle background note in many pops, although they do get their 15 minutes of fame in the Avocado Chile Lime pops (page 95).

The bottom line: Don't be afraid of fat. When it comes to both optimal health and optimal texture for your Glow Pops, fat is not only ideal, but necessary. Just pay attention to the *type* of fat you select, making sure the ones you choose are nourishing your body.

FRUITY

These pops are all about taking in the bounty of beautiful fruit in season during the spring, summer, and fall and letting it shine. *Refreshing* is the primary word that comes to mind, from thirst-quenching Watermelon Lime to spa-ready Cucumber Mint Mojito pops. Because fruit is the star flavor here, it pays to find the best, freshest fruit you can. In the summer, I love to go to farms to pick my own, or hit up my local farmers' market, where the vendors can help me select the highest-quality produce. Ripe fruit will have a powerful, faintly sweet smell that's noticeable even through a rind or peel. To keep more delicate fruit like berries fresh, first pick through to remove any moldy or rotting ones, then soak your remaining berries in a 1:4 mixture of distilled white or apple cider vinegar and water for 10 minutes before rinsing them and laying them out on a clean dishtowel to dry. Once dry, you can store them in the fridge for up to four days—the vinegar bath will have killed any bacteria on their flesh, staving off mold growth.

APPLE PIE

- 2 tablespoons coconut oil

- 5 or 6 apples, unpeeled, cut into 1-inch cubes (about 6 cups)

- ½ cup water

- ½ cup maple syrup or coconut syrup

- 2 teaspoons ground cinnamon

- ½ teaspoon ground ginger

- Generous pinch of salt

Almost all the quercetin (and vitamins) in apples is found in the skin, so if you're consuming apples for their health benefits, be sure not to peel them.

MAKES 5 OR 6 (3-OUNCE) POPS

Recent studies have found that people whose diets regularly include apples actually *do* visit the doctor less. It's likely due to a flavonoid called quercetin, a potent antioxidant that may help protect against heart disease and cancer, in addition to having antihistamine and anti-inflammatory effects. Here they come together with cinnamon and just enough maple or coconut syrup to bring out their natural sweetness. These are a favorite among kids and any other apple pie lovers out there, as they taste just like a big bite of pie filling. You can use any common type of apple here, but I find the sweetness of Fujis and the tartness of Granny Smiths especially pleasing.

1 In a medium pot, melt the coconut oil over medium-high heat. Add the apples and cook, stirring occasionally, for 5 minutes. Reduce the heat to low and add the water, maple syrup, cinnamon, ginger, and salt. Cover and cook for 10 minutes, until the apples are very soft, almost falling apart.

2 Remove from the heat; let the mixture cool until warm to the touch before blending until smooth.

3 Pour the mixture into pop molds and freeze for 1 hour, then insert sticks and freeze for at least 4 hours more, or until solid.

CUCUMBER MINT MOJITO

- 1 medium cucumber, peeled and coarsely chopped

- Zest and juice of 1 lime

- ¼ cup lightly packed fresh mint leaves

- 1 cup water

- 2 tablespoons honey

MAKES 5 OR 6 (3-OUNCE) POPS

The perfect way to cool down and quench your thirst in the midst of summer heat, this pop is all about hydration. Cucumber has the highest water content of any food, and contains an antioxidant called quercetin, which has been found to be anti-inflammatory and bloat-reducing. The lime adds sunscreen-like qualities (citrus zest has been shown to be a skin protectant!) as well as an awesome zip in the flavor, while the mint complements it with an icy burst of refreshment.

1 Blend together all the ingredients until very smooth.

2 Pour the mixture into pop molds and freeze for 1 hour, then insert sticks and freeze for at least 4 hours more, or until solid.

WATERMELON LIME

- 3 cups watermelon, in 1-inch cubes (about 20 ounces)
- Zest and juice of 1 lime

MAKES 5 OR 6 (3-OUNCE) POPS

Is there anything more refreshing than icy-cold watermelon on a hot summer day? There isn't much to this pop, but there doesn't need to be: the zesty acidity of the lime is just enough to brighten the sweet and juicy watermelon. There's a reason we crave watermelons when we're sweating: they're 91 percent water and, therefore, super hydrating. That other 9 percent packs a heavy nutritional punch as well—watermelons contain more lycopene than tomatoes, and an amino acid called L-citrulline that's been found to relieve muscle pain. Fun fact to wow your friends: Did you know watermelon is both a fruit *and* a vegetable, and is a cousin to cucumber, pumpkin, and squash?

1 Blend together all the ingredients until smooth (you can leave some chunks of watermelon if you'd like).

2 Pour the mixture into pop molds and freeze for 1 hour. Insert sticks and freeze for at least 4 hours more, or until solid.

CHAMOMILE CANTALOUPE MINT

- 1 cup water
- ¼ cup coconut sugar
- ½ cup lightly packed fresh mint leaves
- 2 chamomile tea bags, or 2 heaping teaspoons loose-leaf chamomile tea
- ½ large cantaloupe, peeled, seeded, and cut into chunks
- ⅛ teaspoon salt

MAKES 5 OR 6 (3-OUNCE) POPS

This pop is relaxation on a stick, soothing and nourishing at once. I love to use teas in pop recipes, both for their ability to imbue flavor and for their medicinal qualities—and chamomile is no exception. This caffeine-free remedy calms each and every part of your body, from muscle spasms and menstrual cramps to insomnia and anxiety. The mint contributes further tummy-taming properties, while cantaloupe offers a hefty dose of vitamins A and C.

1 In a small pot, bring the water to a boil over high heat. Stir in the coconut sugar, half the mint, and the chamomile, then remove the pot from the heat. Let the mixture steep for 15 minutes, covered, then strain out and discard the mint and chamomile.

2 In a blender, combine the cantaloupe, salt, and chamomile-mint water and blend until very smooth. Finely chop the remaining mint leaves, then pulse them into the cantaloupe mixture until well distributed.

3 Pour the mixture into pop molds and freeze for 1 hour, then insert sticks and freeze for at least 4 hours more, or until solid.

MANGO CHILE

- 2¼ cups cubed fresh mango (from about 2 mangoes)
- ¾ teaspoon chili powder
- Zest and juice of 1 lime
- ⅛ teaspoon salt
- ½ cup water

I've tried this pop with frozen mango and it doesn't work nearly as well—the frozen mango has lost much of the moist juiciness it needs to bring this pop to life.

MAKES 5 OR 6 (3-OUNCE) POPS

I spent much of my childhood in Tucson, Arizona, about an hour from the Mexican border. On the weekends, my friends and I would pile into our parents' cars and head down to Nogales, where we'd bargain for silver and eat way too many Chiclets. My favorite thing about these trips, though, was always the mango sold on the street corners, with a squeeze of lime and a pinch of chili powder. The sweet and juicy mango was offset by the acidic lime and brought to life by the faintly spicy chili powder, and I've captured the same perfect combination in this Glow Pop. Not only do the ingredients balance each other, but they also pack quite a nutritional punch: the mango contains zeaxanthin, an antioxidant that promotes eye health and aids vision; the lime zest offers protection against skin cancer; and the chili powder ramps up your metabolism.

1 Blend together all the ingredients until very smooth.

2 Pour the mixture into pop molds and freeze for 1 hour, then insert sticks and freeze for at least 4 hours more, or until solid.

ROSEMARY STRAWBERRY

- 3 cups hulled fresh strawberries
- ¼ cup water
- 3 sprigs fresh rosemary
- ½ teaspoon pure vanilla extract
- ⅛ teaspoon salt
- 3 tablespoons honey

MAKES 5 OR 6 (3-OUNCE) POPS

While rosemary is typically found in savory dishes, I find its richly woody notes a grounding counterpoint to strawberry's airy sweetness; it infuses this pop with unforgettable flavor. Rosemary is one of the main herbs consumed by residents of so-called blue zones in the Greek islands, named because the people there are among the longest living in the world. Rosemary is powerfully anti-inflammatory and has been found to reduce both the severity and frequency of asthma attacks, while strawberries are rich in vitamin C.

1. In a small pot, combine the strawberries, water, and rosemary and cook over low heat, mushing the strawberries with a wooden spoon, until the berries have collapsed and released their juices, about 10 minutes.

2. Turn off the heat; cover, and let cool for 10 minutes. Remove and discard the rosemary sprigs. Transfer the mixture to a blender and add the vanilla, salt, and honey. Blend until well combined.

3. Pour the mixture into pop molds and freeze for 1 hour, then insert sticks and freeze for at least 4 hours more, or until solid.

HONEYED PEACH THYME

- 4 or 5 medium peaches, halved and pitted
- 3 tablespoons honey
- 1 teaspoon pure vanilla extract
- 1 teaspoon fresh lemon juice
- ⅛ teaspoon salt
- 1 teaspoon fresh thyme leaves

MAKES 5 OR 6 (3-OUNCE) POPS

Thyme's delicately sweet, slightly earthy taste complements rather than overpowers other flavors, and adds a subtle depth and uniqueness. It's also antiviral and antibacterial, and has been used for centuries to ward off everything from simple coughs to the plague. In fact, whenever I feel like I'm getting sick, I'll steep some fresh thyme in a cup of hot water and inhale the steam before drinking the resulting herbal tisane—and often, I'll find I'm better by the next morning. Here I've paired the herb with fresh summer peaches, roasted in the oven to concentrate their sweetness.

1   Preheat the oven to 350°F. Place the peaches cut-side down on a rimmed baking sheet and bake for 20 minutes. Remove from the oven and let rest for 10 minutes, until cool to the touch.

2   Transfer the peaches, skin still on, to a blender or food processor and add the honey, vanilla, lemon juice, and salt. Blend until mostly smooth. Add the thyme and blend for 1 minute more to incorporate.

3   Pour the mixture into pop molds and freeze for 1 hour, then insert sticks and freeze for at least 4 hours more, or until solid.

PINK LEMONADE

- ¾ cup fresh lemon juice (from 4 or 5 lemons)
- ⅓ cup honey
- 1½ cups fresh or frozen raspberries

MAKES 5 OR 6 (3-OUNCE) POPS

Pink lemonade is always so much better than the regular kind, isn't it? There's something superior about the sweetness of raspberries contrasted with the tartness of the lemon—that, and the aesthetic appeal of pretty bright pink, of course. Raspberries are one of the most fiber-filled fruits, meaning they'll help keep you regular and eliminate bloating, while lemon helps support your liver, the body's natural detoxifier. But for me, these pops are all about the flavor—they're just the refreshing, juicy hit I crave on a hot day.

1 Blend together all the ingredients until smooth.

2 Pour the mixture into pop molds and freeze for 1 hour, then insert sticks and freeze for at least 4 hours more, or until solid.

LAVENDER BLUEBERRY

- ½ cup water
- 1 cup coconut sugar
- 1 tablespoon dried culinary lavender (see page 21)
- 4 cups fresh blueberries

MAKES 5 OR 6 (3-OUNCE) POPS

My friend Nicola has a theory that foods of similar colors will often taste delicious together. I don't know how well this applies to, say, white chocolate and cauliflower, but here it works brilliantly. Lavender adds a delicate floral note to the sweet and tart blueberries. Lavender has been used for thousands of years to soothe both the body and the mind, for everything from ailments of the digestive tract to anxiety. Blueberries are well known for their superfood status, and have been proven to lower blood pressure, support heart health, and help cell regeneration and brain protection, with recent studies even pointing to their ability to stave off Alzheimer's!

1 In a small saucepan, whisk together the water and coconut sugar. Bring to a boil over medium heat, then reduce the heat to medium-low and simmer for 10 minutes, until the mixture begins to thicken. Add the lavender and simmer for 10 minutes more, until the mixture has reduced by about half and looks thick and syrupy. Remove the pot from the heat and strain through a fine-mesh strainer into a bowl. Discard the lavender. Let the syrup cool for 15 minutes. Transfer the syrup to a food processor, add the blueberries, and process until very smooth.

2 Pour the mixture into pop molds and freeze for 1 hour, then insert sticks and freeze for at least 4 hours more, or until solid.

BLACKBERRY ROSE

- 6 cups fresh blackberries

- 1 tablespoon rose water (see page 21)

- 1 teaspoon pure vanilla extract

- 1 teaspoon fresh lemon juice

- ¼ cup honey

- ⅛ teaspoon salt

MAKES 5 OR 6 (3-OUNCE) POPS

Ah, rose—how I do love thee. While rose water is found commonly in Middle Eastern and Indian dishes, it's more of a rarity in the United States—but it shouldn't be. Besides having a delicate floral flavor that complements the juicy blackberries in this recipe, rose water is rich in flavonoids, antioxidants, tannins, and essential vitamins like A, C, D, E, and B3. It's also a mild relaxant and mood balancer—even just the aroma is known to calm a restless or stressed mind. It's made by steam-distilling fresh rose petals and can be found in the international section of most grocery stores, Indian or Middle Eastern markets, and many liquor stores (as it's a common ingredient in cocktails). This pop oozes sophistication, and is a lovely go-to when you want something outside the norm.

1   Place all the ingredients in a food processor and pulse until smooth.

2   Pour the mixture into pop molds and freeze for 1 hour, then insert sticks and freeze for at least 4 hours more, or until solid.

CARAMELIZED PINEAPPLE

- 2 tablespoons coconut oil or ghee

- ¼ cup coconut sugar

- 5 cups fresh pineapple, in 1-inch chunks (about 1 medium pineapple)

- ⅛ teaspoon salt

If you want to grill the pineapple instead of sautéing it, cut your pineapple lengthwise into 5 or 6 long strips. Rub with the coconut oil and sprinkle with coconut sugar before placing directly on a grill that has been heated to 400 degrees. Sear until grill marks appear, 2 to 3 minutes per side, before letting it cool completely and transferring it to a food processor. Follow the rest of the recipe as instructed.

MAKES 5 OR 6 (3-OUNCE) POPS

Pineapple is truly the best thing to barbecue—the heat caramelizes the fruit, deepening its flavor in a way that's truly mind-blowing. This recipe allows you to capture this summer sensation even if you don't have access to a grill, as cooking the pineapple on the stovetop creates the same Maillard reaction. Pineapples are one of my favorite healthy foods, as they're the only natural source of bromelain, a digestive enzyme so potent that many people supplement their diets with it. This makes these pops the perfect accompaniment to a summer feast, as it'll help your body digest whatever else you eat and eliminate bloat before you hit the pool later.

1 In large sauté pan, melt the coconut oil over high heat. Sprinkle the coconut sugar generously all over the pineapple, then add the pineapple to the pan and sear, stirring frequently, until rich brown on all sides, about 10 minutes.

2 Let cool completely before transferring the pineapple to a food processor. Add the salt and process until smooth.

3 Pour the mixture into pop molds and freeze for 1 hour, then insert sticks and freeze for at least 4 hours more, or until solid.

CREAMY

COCONUT CHAI 49

CINNAMON ORANGE
& CREAM 50

STRAWBERRY CARDAMOM
ROSE LASSI 51

MEXICAN HORCHATA 52

COOKIE DOUGH 53

BLUEBERRY & CREAM 55

MATCHA LATTE 56

TURMERIC GOLDEN MILK 59

PEANUT BUTTER & JELLY 60

LAVENDER LONDON FOG 63

WHITE CHOCOLATE CHIA
STRAWBERRY 65

These pops will take you around the world, from grassy Japanese matcha tea to a healthier take on a cinnamon-y Mexican Horchata to Indian Turmeric Golden Milk, an Ayurvedic remedy that's been used to bolster the immune system for thousands of years. The secret to a creamy pop is all in the base. For most of the recipes in this chapter, I like to use full-fat canned coconut milk, which will give you that perfect, smooth result. Light canned coconut milk also works well, albeit with slightly less creamy results, and the homemade milks included in Getting Started (see page 17) are good choices, too. Whatever you do, don't use store-bought nut milks, as they're generally much too thin and will result in a watery, icy pop (see page 15 for more information).

COCONUT CHAI

- 2 cups full-fat coconut milk

- 10 cardamom pods, gently crushed

- 1 (1½-inch) piece fresh ginger, peeled and sliced

- 2 cinnamon sticks

- ¼ teaspoon whole cloves

- ½ teaspoon fennel seeds

- ¼ teaspoon whole black peppercorns

- 3 tablespoons coconut sugar

- 1 teaspoon pure vanilla extract

- 2 black tea bags

MAKES 5 OR 6 (3-OUNCE) POPS

Generally, chai is a specific blend of black tea, spices, milk, and sweetener. The spices vary in type and amount (some families guard their chai recipe with their lives), but tend to include cinnamon, cardamom, cloves, black peppercorns, and ginger. I've swapped the traditional dairy for coconut milk, which is commonly used in Indian cooking and plays beautifully with the mélange of spices. All the spices here are health superstars as well: cinnamon balances blood sugar, fennel and ginger soothe the stomach and decrease bloat, black pepper helps increase absorption of other nutrients and helps burn fat, and cloves are highly antibacterial. This pop does contain caffeine from the black tea, but you can replace it with caffeine-free rooibos tea if you prefer.

1   In a medium saucepan, combine all the ingredients except the tea bags. Bring to a boil over medium-high heat, then reduce the heat to low, cover, and simmer for 30 minutes. Turn off the heat, add the tea bags, and steep, covered, for 5 minutes more. Remove and discard the tea bags. Let the mixture cool for 20 minutes, then pour it through a fine-mesh strainer into a bowl. Discard any solids left in the strainer.

2   Pour the mixture into pop molds and freeze for 1 hour, then insert sticks and freeze for at least 4 hours more, or until solid.

CINNAMON ORANGE & CREAM

- 1 cup full-fat coconut milk
- Zest and juice of 2 oranges
- 3 tablespoons honey
- 2 teaspoons ground cinnamon
- 1 teaspoon pure vanilla extract
- ⅛ teaspoon salt

MAKES 5 OR 6 (3-OUNCE) POPS

I first discovered the combination of cinnamon and orange in a tiny village in Morocco, where orange slices were served with a sprinkle of the spice on top. Seemingly simple, it's become one of my favorite flavor profiles—the cinnamon lends a spicy, aromatic quality while bringing out the zesty freshness of the orange, and the sweetness of each teases and complements the other. Cinnamon is a wonder spice: numerous studies point to its ability to stabilize blood sugar, lower LDL (or "bad") cholesterol, fight fungal and bacterial infections, and even protect against cancer. Oranges are vitamin C powerhouses, making your skin glow and helping keep your immune system in top-notch shape. If you'd prefer the taste of the classic Creamsicle of your childhood, simply omit the cinnamon.

1 Blend together all the ingredients until very smooth.

2 Pour the mixture into pop molds and freeze for 1 hour, then insert sticks and freeze for at least 4 hours more, or until solid.

STRAWBERRY CARDAMOM ROSE LASSI

- 1 cup hulled and halved fresh strawberries

- ¾ cup unsweetened yogurt (coconut, Greek, and full-fat regular all work well)

- 3 Medjool dates, pitted, soaked in boiling water for 10 minutes, and drained

- 1 teaspoon rose water (see page 21)

- 1 teaspoon ground cardamom

- 1 teaspoon pure vanilla extract

MAKES 5 OR 6 (3-OUNCE) POPS

Lassis are popular drinks in Indian cuisine, typically made with some type of fruit (mango is common) blended with sugar and yogurt to make a creamy, refreshing concoction. Here I elevated the traditional flavors to something slightly more exotic, with a blend of strawberry and rose that's downright transporting. Rose water is made by steam-distilling fresh rose petals and has a delicately sweet flavor. It's rich in vitamins A and C, which boost collagen and increase cell turnover in your skin, making it glow. It's also known for its relaxing properties—just a whiff is often enough to calm me down! No matter which kind of yogurt you use, it will provide a hefty dose of probiotics, which have been linked to clearer skin, reduced anxiety, and weight loss.

1 Blend together all the ingredients until very smooth.

2 Pour the mixture into pop molds and freeze for 1 hour, then insert sticks and freeze for at least 4 hours more, or until solid.

MEXICAN HORCHATA

- 2 cups full-fat coconut milk

- 6 Medjool dates, pitted, soaked in boiling water for 10 minutes, and drained

- 1 tablespoon ground cinnamon

- 1 teaspoon pure vanilla extract

- Pinch of salt

MAKES 5 OR 6 (3-OUNCE) POPS

I'm obsessed with horchata, a sweet Mexican drink traditionally made with rice milk and cinnamon. To avoid the icy texture rice milk takes on when frozen, I swapped it out for coconut milk to make a creamy, dreamy pop with a perfect texture. Cinnamon stokes your metabolism and helps balance blood sugar, and I've long been a fan of dates' ability to mimic caramel, with a rich and buttery sweetness that works perfectly with the warmth of the cinnamon. Plus, they're rich in fiber and potassium. The ingredients here are simple but utterly unexpected. This recipe often winds up being people's favorite Glow Pop!

1 Blend together all the ingredients until very smooth.

2 Pour the mixture into pop molds and freeze for 1 hour, then insert sticks and freeze for at least 4 hours more, or until solid.

COOKIE DOUGH

- 1½ cups raw cashews, soaked for 1 to 2 hours, then drained

- 1 tablespoon pure vanilla extract

- 1½ tablespoons smooth almond butter

- ¼ teaspoon salt

- ⅓ cup honey

- 1 cup water

- ½ cup raw cacao nibs or mini chocolate chips

You can use raw or roasted almond butter in this recipe— the roasted version will give a slightly richer flavor.

MAKES 5 OR 6 (3-OUNCE) POPS

I'm definitely one of those people who prefers cookie dough to actual cookies, so these pops always hit the spot—but in a much healthier way! The secret is in the mix of rich cashews and almond butter that come together to create that creamy, buttery texture that chocolate chip cookie dough is famous for. Almonds are rich in vitamin E, protein, and heart-healthy fat, while cashews contain largely heart-healthy monounsaturated fats, with a hefty dose of skin-beautifying copper to boot. Honey adds a lovely sweetness, while pure vanilla extract adds that just-out-of-the-oven aroma. I love to make these with raw cacao nibs, which offer potent antioxidants and a bitter, rich chocolate flavor that offsets the creamy sweetness, but they'd also be great with mini chocolate chips.

1 Blend together all the ingredients except the cacao nibs until very smooth. Add the nibs and pulse until just combined.

2 Pour the mixture into pop molds and freeze for 1 hour, then insert sticks and freeze for at least 4 hours more, or until solid.

BLUEBERRY & CREAM

- 1 cup full-fat coconut milk

- ¼ cup honey

- 1 teaspoon pure vanilla extract

- ⅛ teaspoon salt

- ¾ cup frozen or fresh blueberries

I like to use frozen blueberries in this recipe because they're much smaller, allowing you to more easily suspend them within the coconut milk "cream." Plus, they're generally cheaper than fresh, and available all year round. Fresh wild blueberries also work wonderfully.

MAKES 5 OR 6 (3-OUNCE) POPS

These pops are just so pretty, with bright, colorful blueberries dotting a creamy white background like they're nature's confetti. I love not blending the cream with the blueberries, so they remain evenly suspended throughout the cream mixture and you get the separation of the sweet milkiness and the tart, juicy blueberries in every bite. Blueberries are one of those health foods that have garnered a reputation as a superfood, and for good reason. They have the highest antioxidant capacity of any commonly consumed fruit or vegetable, resulting in protection against heart disease and cell damage. They've also been shown to help increase memory function and prevent cognitive decline, and their compounds are currently being studied as a potential remedy for Alzheimer's. Similar to cranberries, they're also effective in preventing and treating UTIs.

1 Blend together the milk, honey, vanilla, and salt until smooth.

2 Spoon half the blueberries into pop molds, dividing them evenly. Top with the cream mixture, filling the molds about three-quarters of the way, then add the remaining blueberries. Fill any remaining space in the molds with a very small amount of the cream.

3 Freeze for 1 hour, then insert sticks and freeze for at least 4 hours more, or until solid.

MATCHA LATTE

- 2 cups full-fat coconut milk

- 2 teaspoons matcha powder

- 3 tablespoons sweetener of choice (see page 12)

MAKES 5 OR 6 (3-OUNCE) POPS

Matcha has taken the health food world by storm in recent years, and I must confess I haven't been immune to its charms. Fancy ceremonial rituals aside, matcha is simply finely ground green tea. Instead of steeping it and discarding the leaves, you dissolve the whole-leaf powder in whatever liquid you're using and drink it. Because you're consuming the whole tea leaf, rather than simply infusing liquid with it, the health benefits skyrocket: matcha has 137 more antioxidants than regularly brewed green tea, including EGCG, which has been found in numerous studies to have potent cancer-fighting properties. This pop has a slightly grassy, sweet flavor that will quickly become addictive.

1 Blend together all the ingredients until smooth.

2 Pour the mixture into pop molds and freeze for 1 hour, then insert sticks and freeze for at least 4 hours more, or until solid.

TURMERIC GOLDEN MILK

- 2 cups full-fat coconut milk

- 3 tablespoons honey

- 1 teaspoon ground turmeric

- 1 teaspoon ground ginger

- ⅛ teaspoon freshly ground black pepper

If you're an allergy sufferer like me, use local honey when you make this pop. Between the anti-inflammatory action of the turmeric and the local honey inoculating you against nearby pollens, your runny nose and itchy eyes will be gone in no time.

MAKES 5 OR 6 (3-OUNCE) POPS

Long prized as a healing elixir in Ayurvedic tradition, turmeric golden milk is a mixture of turmeric, milk, and sweetener, and is typically drunk warm. It's one of my favorite winter beverages: the turmeric is earthy, the ginger and black pepper add a hint of spice, and the honey and coconut milk ground it all in creamy sweetness. All the healthy properties shine in a Glow Pop form. The superstar is turmeric, which is prized for its anti-inflammatory benefits and has been shown in numerous studies to match or even outperform over-the-counter NSAIDs. Some studies have also shown turmeric's effectiveness in treating conditions like IBS, rheumatoid arthritis, cystic fibrosis, and even cancer. Always be sure to consume turmeric with both black pepper and fat, as they make the spice 150 percent more bioavailable, dramatically increasing its healthful effects in your body.

1 Blend together all the ingredients until smooth.

2 Pour the mixture into pop molds and freeze for 1 hour, then insert sticks and freeze for at least 4 hours more, or until solid.

PEANUT BUTTER & JELLY

JELLY LAYER

- 4 cups frozen raspberries
- 2 teaspoons pure vanilla extract
- 2 teaspoons honey
- Pinch of salt
- 2 tablespoons chia seeds

PEANUT BUTTER LAYER

- ¾ cup canned coconut milk or homemade milk of choice
- ½ cup peanut butter (creamy and crunchy both work well)
- 3 tablespoons honey

MAKES 5 OR 6 (3-OUNCE) POPS

This pop evokes childhood in such a playful way while looking super grown-up—the swirls of smooth tan peanut butter and chia seed-studded raspberry jelly are absolutely stunning. Chia seeds are one of my favorite ingredients to make a quick and easy jelly, thanks to their seemingly magic ability to make any liquid thick and gelatinous (see page 24). They're incredibly filling and full of fiber, protein, and good fat. Here they're swirled with protein- and vitamin E-filled peanut butter for a sweet-and-salty combo that's equally good for breakfast, a light lunch, or dessert.

1 Make the jelly layer: In a small saucepan, cook the frozen raspberries over low heat, squishing and stirring them with a wooden spoon, for 10 to 15 minutes, until they defrost and release their juices. Remove from the heat and stir in the vanilla, honey, and salt. Sprinkle the chia seeds over the mixture, then stir to combine. Let sit for 15 to 20 minutes, or until the mixture becomes jelly-like.

(recipe continues)

Any leftover raspberry jelly can be spread on toast, spooned onto oatmeal or ice cream, or eaten plain for a quick energy boost!

2 Meanwhile, make the peanut butter layer: Blend together all the ingredients until smooth (or with a bit of texture, if you're using crunchy peanut butter).

3 Place a teaspoon of the peanut butter mixture in the tip of each mold, then add a few spoonfuls of the jelly mixture. Continue to alternate peanut butter and jelly until your molds are full. If you'd like a swirled look, stir a chopstick or knife through the mixture once, until peanut butter and jelly layers are swirled but not fully mixed.

4 Freeze for 1 hour, then insert sticks and freeze for at least 4 hours more, or until solid.

LAVENDER LONDON FOG

- 2 cups full-fat coconut milk

- 3 tablespoons coconut sugar

- 3 Earl Grey tea bags or 1 tablespoon loose-leaf Earl Grey tea

- 1 teaspoon dried culinary lavender (see page 21)

- ½ teaspoon pure vanilla extract

MAKES 5 OR 6 (3-OUNCE) POPS

Essentially an Earl Grey latte, a London Fog's milky sweetness perfectly complements bitter orange bergamot and tannic black tea. Here, I upped the ante even further by adding lavender, which makes the entire pop taste surprising, luxurious, and perfectly balanced. Black tea has been found to ward off certain types of cancer, reduce the risk of stroke and type 2 diabetes, and defend against heart disease. Combined with calming, anti-inflammatory lavender, it's a perfect wellness elixir.

1 In a small pot, bring the milk just to a boil over medium-high heat, then immediately remove from the heat. Stir in the coconut sugar until dissolved, then add the tea and the lavender. Cover and steep for 10 minutes.

2 Pour the mixture through a fine-mesh strainer into a bowl. Discard the tea and lavender. Stir in the vanilla. Let the mixture cool to room temperature, about 15 minutes, then stir.

3 Pour the mixture into pop molds and freeze for 1 hour, then insert sticks and freeze for at least 4 hours more, or until solid.

You can use cocoa butter in place of the cacao butter if you prefer. They're essentially the same thing, but cocoa butter has been processed at higher temperatures, causing it to lose some of its antioxidants.

WHITE CHOCOLATE CHIA STRAWBERRY

- 2 tablespoons cacao butter

- 4 Medjool dates, pitted, soaked in boiling water for 10 minutes, and drained

- 1 cup canned coconut milk or homemade milk of choice

- 1 teaspoon pure vanilla extract

- ⅛ teaspoon salt

- 3 tablespoons chia seeds

- 2 cups hulled fresh strawberries

- ¼ cup water

MAKES 5 OR 6 (3-OUNCE) POPS

This pop is one of my favorite summer breakfasts—the good fats and fiber in the chia seeds and strawberries offer more than enough substance to power me through to lunch. Cacao butter, the pressed oil of the cacao bean, creates the white chocolate flavor. Like cacao powder and nibs, both long recognized as superfoods, the butter is rich in antioxidants; oleic acid, which has been shown to reduce the risk of heart disease; and theobromine, which raises energy and alertness levels.

1 In a small saucepan, melt the cacao butter over low heat, stirring frequently. Transfer to a blender; add the dates, milk, vanilla, and salt; and blend until very smooth.

2 Place the chia seeds in a large glass jar or container, then pour the milk mixture over them. Stir thoroughly, then let sit for 30 minutes until set into a gel. Meanwhile, puree the strawberries in a blender until smooth, adding water 1 tablespoon at a time as necessary to reach the desired texture.

3 In alternating layers, fill the molds with the chia mixture and strawberry puree. Freeze for 1 hour, then insert sticks and freeze for at least 4 hours more, or until solid.

CH

OCOLATEY

Is there anything better than a frozen chocolate treat on a hot summer's day . . . or really, anytime? These Glow Pops allow you to enjoy your sweets and nourish yourself, too, forgoing the heavily processed chocolate of typical desserts for raw cacao, a pure form of the cacao bean that's regarded as a superfood packed with vitamins, minerals, and antioxidants (see page 22). From the Chocolate Fudge pop, which uses avocado to mimic the creamy texture of the childhood favorite Fudgsicle, to the decidedly more grown-up Olive Oil Chocolate Rosemary to the decadent Chocolate Caramel Swirl that will surprise everyone with its secret, healthy ingredient, these chocolate pops are easy wins with any crowd, whether you're interested in health or not.

MEXICAN HOT CHOCOLATE

- 1½ cups full-fat coconut milk
- ¼ cup maple syrup
- 2 teaspoons ground cinnamon
- 6 tablespoons raw cacao powder
- ¼ teaspoon freshly grated nutmeg
- ⅛ teaspoon cayenne
- 1 teaspoon pure vanilla extract
- ⅛ teaspoon salt

MAKES 5 OR 6 (3-OUNCE) POPS

Mexican hot chocolate is one of my favorite flavor combinations: sweet chocolate with spicy chiles and warm cinnamon. I'm guilty of trying it in everything from green smoothies to energy balls to pancakes. I often find myself staring wistfully at plain chocolate bars, wondering why they're so naked and spiceless. Spices are the built-in superfoods of any kitchen cabinet, so punching up the flavor punches up the nutrition factor as well. Cinnamon helps keep your blood sugar stable, making it a great option for anyone with blood sugar issues. Cayenne boosts your metabolism, and nutmeg contains specific antimicrobial compounds that work to freshen breath (yes, that is permission to eat one of these before that important meeting!). A word of warning: Once you try this kicked-up version of chocolate, you'll never want to go back to the basic stuff again.

1 Blend together all the ingredients until very smooth.

2 Pour the mixture into pop molds and freeze for 1 hour, then insert sticks and freeze for at least 4 hours more, or until solid.

CHOCOLATE FUDGE

- ¾ cup full-fat coconut milk

- 1 ripe avocado, pitted and peeled

- 6 tablespoons raw cacao powder

- 1 teaspoon pure vanilla extract

- 4 Medjool dates, pitted, soaked in boiling water for 10 minutes, and drained

- 2 tablespoons honey

- ¼ teaspoon salt

MAKES 5 OR 6 (3-OUNCE) POPS

This pop tastes exactly like a Fudgsicle. The trick is in the texture: you want that super-creamy, easy-to-bite, ice-free consistency. I accomplish that here with a secret ingredient: avocado. While the strong chocolate flavor hides any hint of avocado taste, its inclusion creates that perfect smoothness you remember from childhood—but without the chemical nasties, and with plenty of good fats to nourish your skin and hair. Full-fat coconut milk adds to the texture, and a dose of antioxidant-rich cacao powder ensures a rich, chocolatey flavor.

1 Blend together all the ingredients until very smooth; the mixture should have the consistency of pudding. If it becomes too thick, add water 1 tablespoon at a time as needed to thin it.

2 Pour the mixture into pop molds and tap them on the counter to remove any air bubbles. Freeze for 1 hour, then insert sticks and freeze for at least 4 hours more, or until solid.

CHOCOLATE-COVERED BANANA

BANANA POPS

- 3 ripe bananas
- 1 cup canned coconut milk or homemade milk of choice
- 1 teaspoon pure vanilla extract
- ⅛ teaspoon salt

CHOCOLATE SHELL

- 6 ounces coarsely chopped dark chocolate
- ¼ cup coconut oil

To melt chocolate using a microwave, place the chopped chocolate in a wide, shallow bowl. Microwave in 15- to 20-second intervals, stirring between each, until the chocolate is completely melted and smooth.

MAKES 5 OR 6 (3-OUNCE) POPS

In healthy cooking, bananas are a superstar fruit, pulling weight to hold together pancake batter and to sweeten and add creaminess to smoothies and pops (you'll see them in many of the green pops). They've even been turned into soft-serve ice cream! After so many supporting roles, they get their turn as the star here, in a pop that highlights their creamy sweetness by draping it in a decadent chocolate shell. Besides being one of the cheapest fruits on the market (I once bought six bananas for less than $1), bananas are rich in potassium, fiber, and vitamin C. Be sure to let them ripen completely before using them—brown spots mean their starch has converted into sugar, making the fruit easier to digest, more blendable, and better tasting!

1 Make the pops: Blend together all the ingredients until very smooth.

2 Pour the mixture into pop molds and freeze for 1 hour, then insert sticks and freeze for at least 4 hours more, or until solid.

(recipe continues)

To melt chocolate on the stovetop, heat 2 to 3 inches of water in a medium saucepan over medium heat until it's boiling. Place a tightly fitting bowl on top—make sure the bottom of the bowl doesn't touch the water and no steam can escape from the sides where the bowl meets the saucepan. Add the chopped chocolate to the bowl and stir frequently, until the chocolate is completely melted and smooth.

3 Once completely frozen, unmold the pops and lay them on a parchment- or waxed paper–lined plate or baking sheet. Store them in the freezer while you make the chocolate shell.

4 Make the chocolate shell: Melt the chocolate (see Tips at left and on page 71) until completely liquid. Stir in the coconut oil until the mixture is very smooth, then let it sit for 5 to 10 minutes, or until it's still liquid but cool enough to touch.

5 Remove the pops from the freezer. Working quickly, dip each frozen pop into the chocolate, twisting the pop around to coat evenly. Alternatively, drizzle the chocolate shell over the pops in a fun pattern for a festive touch.

6 Return the chocolate-covered pops to the plate or baking sheet and freeze until ready to eat.

CHOCOLATE HAZELNUT

- 2 cups raw hazelnuts
- ⅛ teaspoon salt, plus a pinch
- 2 cups water
- 3 tablespoons raw cacao powder
- 3 tablespoons maple syrup

The base of this pop is essentially a very creamy Nutella-flavored milk, which I also love to drink straight or, if I'm feeling really decadent, pour over a bowl of granola or cereal.

MAKES 5 OR 6 (3-OUNCE) POPS

I became addicted to Nutella the first time I went to Europe. With little effort, the creamy spread proved that chocolate and hazelnut are the perfect flavor combination. This Chocolate Hazelnut pop takes the best of Nutella, keeping its healthy, whole-food ingredients and leaving out the less desirable processed ones. Hazelnuts are no slouch in the health department, boasting the most folate of any tree nut (for all you expectant mamas out there, that's your excuse to eat as many of these pops as you'd like), plus high quantities of skin- and hair-beautifying manganese and copper. Soaking the nuts overnight makes them easier to blend, as well as decreases the quantity of phytic acid, which impedes mineral absorption in the body.

1   Soak the hazelnuts in water to cover with a pinch of salt for 12 hours, then drain and transfer to a blender. Add the remaining ingredients and blend until very smooth. If desired, let sit for 30 minutes to allow the foam and air bubbles to dissipate.

2   Pour the mixture into pop molds and freeze for 1 hour, then insert sticks and freeze for at least 4 hours more, or until solid.

COLD-BREW MOCHA

- ¾ cup full-fat coconut milk
- ¾ cup undiluted cold-brew coffee concentrate
- ¼ cup coconut syrup (see page 14)
- 1 tablespoon raw cacao powder

MAKES 5 OR 6 (3-OUNCE) POPS

For those days when you wish your coffee could just make itself, now you can just grab a mocha pop from the freezer and go! Chocolate and coffee are a classic combination—plus, this recipe utilizes cold-brew coffee for an extra health boost. Cold-brew coffee is, as the name suggests, brewed for twelve to twenty-four hours in *cold* water, rather than by the typical hot water–steeping method. It is less bitter and acidic than traditional coffee (by as much as 67 percent), and highly concentrated. Coffee—cold brew or otherwise—is also rich in antioxidants, magnesium, and chromium, and has been found in studies to reduce the risk of type 2 diabetes as well as Alzheimer's. You can find cold-brew coffee in the refrigerated section at most grocery stores, or you can make it yourself (see recipe at right).

1 Blend together all the ingredients until very smooth.

2 Pour the mixture into pop molds and freeze for 1 hour, then insert sticks and freeze for at least 4 hours more, or until solid.

MAKE YOUR OWN
COLD-BREW COFFEE

MAKES 2 CUPS

- 1 cup coarsely ground coffee beans
- 2 cups filtered water

In a large bowl or glass jar, stir together the ground coffee beans and water. Cover and refrigerate for 12 to 24 hours. Strain the mixture into another bowl or jar by pouring it through a fine-mesh strainer lined with a traditional coffee filter or cheesecloth. Discard the coffee grounds. You can store any leftover cold-brew coffee in a covered container or jar in the fridge. To drink, rather than use in pops, dilute with 2 cups water for every 1 cup of cold brew.

NEAPOLITAN

- 1½ cups frozen strawberries

- ⅓ cup plus 1¼ cups full-fat coconut milk

- 5½ tablespoons chia seeds

- ⅛ teaspoon salt

- 2 teaspoons vanilla bean powder (or pure vanilla extract)

- 2½ tablespoons plus 1¼ teaspoons honey

- 4 teaspoons raw cacao powder

MAKES 5 OR 6 (3-OUNCE) POPS

Neapolitan ice cream technically refers to the combination of several flavors. The original version from Naples was usually more like spumoni, with pistachio, chocolate, and cherry or strawberry ice cream, but this recipe riffs off the American classic flavor combination: smooth and buttery vanilla, sweet and fruity strawberry, and rich chocolate. Chia seeds are the secret that allows this pop's layers to remain distinct, while also adding tons of fiber, protein, and good fat. I love to use chia seeds in pop recipes because they give the pops a creamy, almost gelato-like texture, and these are no exception—the final result is as decadent as a childhood ice cream sandwich. Strawberries, beyond being the pretty, fruity counter to the vanilla and chocolate, are rich in vitamin C, which helps create skin-boosting collagen. You can put aside any leftover strawberry compote to use as an oatmeal or toast topping, or mix chia seeds into it to make a jam.

1   In a small saucepan, cook the strawberries over low heat, breaking them up with the back of a wooden spoon, for about 20 minutes, or until completely thawed. Bring to a simmer and cook, stirring occasionally, for 10 minutes more.

(recipe continues)

Want to keep your layers distinct and your pops looking perfect? The easiest way to make sure the mixture doesn't scrape the sides is to pour each one into a zip-top bag or a piping bag, then cut off the tip and squeeze the mixture into the center of the mold. This is only for appearances, to keep the colors totally separate—feel free to skip it.

2 Transfer ⅓ cup of the strawberry compote to a small bowl and add the ⅓ cup milk and 2 tablespoons of the chia seeds. In a separate small bowl, stir together the remaining 1¼ cups milk and 3½ tablespoons chia seeds. Let both sit for 15 minutes, or until a thick gel forms.

3 Transfer the milk-chia mixture to a blender. Add half the salt, 1½ teaspoons of the vanilla, and the 2½ tablespoons honey. Blend until smooth, stopping to scrape down the sides of the blender as needed. Set aside half the mixture. Add the cacao powder to the mixture in the blender and blend until combined. Transfer to a bowl and rinse out the blender.

4 Blend together the strawberry-chia mixture and the remaining 1¼ teaspoons honey, salt, and ½ teaspoon vanilla extract until smooth.

5 Spoon the chocolate mixture into each pop mold until it is one-third full, then add the strawberry mixture until the molds are two-thirds full, and fill the remaining space in the molds with the vanilla mixture. Tap the molds on the counter between each layer to remove any air bubbles.

6 Freeze for 1 hour, then insert sticks and freeze for 6 hours more or overnight, until solid.

CHOCOLATE ORANGE

- 1 cup full-fat coconut milk

- Zest and juice of 2 oranges

- 3 tablespoons honey

- 6 tablespoons raw cacao powder

- 1 teaspoon pure vanilla extract

- ⅛ teaspoon salt

MAKES 5 OR 6 (3-OUNCE) POPS

When I was a child, I'd rush downstairs every Christmas to find a chocolate orange stuffed into the tip of my stocking. It was the type you had to smash against a hard surface to reveal a dozen slim wedges—and it was the beginning of my love affair with this flavor combination. Can you blame me? Rich, creamy dark chocolate beautifully complements the zesty brightness of orange. While chocolate you find in the store is highly processed and so far removed from the cacao bean that many of the precious antioxidants and minerals are destroyed, raw cacao is one of the purest forms. I personally love it for the steady energy it gives (much gentler than caffeine) and the simultaneous calming effect of the magnesium it contains. This pop is also packed with vitamin C, of course, but by using the orange *zest*, we amp up the flavor, add additional antioxidants, and protect against skin cancer.

1 Blend together all the ingredients until very smooth.

2 Pour the mixture into pop molds and freeze for 1 hour, then insert sticks and freeze for at least 4 hours more, or until solid.

PEANUT BUTTER CUP

PEANUT BUTTER POPS

- 1 ¼ cups canned coconut milk or homemade milk of choice
- ⅔ cup peanut butter (creamy and crunchy both work well)
- ⅛ teaspoon salt
- 3 tablespoons honey

CHOCOLATE SHELL

- 6 ounces coarsely chopped dark chocolate
- ¼ cup coconut oil

MAKES 5 OR 6 (3-OUNCE) POPS

Peanut butter cups were my absolute favorite childhood candy—I remember rifling through my plastic pumpkin every Halloween so I could eat them all first. There's something about the combination of salty peanut butter and smooth, rich chocolate that sends my taste buds to high heaven—and with these pops, I get all the pleasure with none of the artificial flavors, high-fructose corn syrup, or unhealthy fat. Peanut butter, when consumed in its whole state, is actually quite healthy—full of good fats, protein, and skin-boosting vitamin E. Here, a creamy peanut butter pop hides inside a dark chocolate shell for a show-stopping treat that's as decadent as a candy bar. Just be sure to look for peanut butter with only one ingredient—peanuts—and no highly processed oils or additives.

1 Make the peanut butter pops: Blend together all the peanut butter pop ingredients until very smooth (or with some texture, if using crunchy peanut butter).

2 Pour the mixture into pop molds and freeze for 1 hour, then insert sticks and freeze for at least 4 hours more, or until solid. Once completely frozen, unmold the pops and lay them on a parchment- or waxed paper–lined plate or baking sheet and store in the freezer while you make the chocolate shell.

3 Make the chocolate shell: Melt the chocolate (see Tips, pages 71 and 72) until completely liquid. Stir in the coconut oil until the mixture is very smooth, then let it sit for 5 to 10 minutes, or until it's still liquid but cool enough to touch.

4 Remove the pops from the freezer. Working quickly, dip each frozen pop into the chocolate, twisting the pop around to coat evenly. Alternatively, drizzle the chocolate shell over the pops in a fun pattern for a festive touch.

5 Return the chocolate-covered pops to the plate or baking sheet and freeze until ready to eat.

CHOCOLATE CHIA LAVENDER

- 1¾ cups canned coconut milk or homemade milk of choice

- 1 tablespoon dried culinary lavender (see page 21)

- 6 Medjool dates, pitted, soaked in boiling water for 10 minutes, and drained

- 1 teaspoon pure vanilla extract

- ¼ cup raw cacao powder

- ⅛ teaspoon salt

- ¼ cup chia seeds

MAKES 5 OR 6 (3-OUNCE) POPS

In this pop, the richness of the chocolate is heightened by the lavender notes—an unexpected twist. Lavender has long been renowned for its ability to soothe both body and mind, and is used as a remedy for anxiety, depression, insomnia, restlessness, in stomachaches, and indigestion. Loaded with omega-3s, fiber, and protein-rich chia seeds as well as antioxidant-packed raw cacao powder, this pop makes a great healthy dessert, and is filling enough to be a hearty breakfast.

1 In a medium pot, bring the milk to a boil over medium-high heat, then remove from the heat and add the lavender. Cover and steep for 20 minutes. Pour the mixture through a fine-mesh strainer into the blender. Discard the lavender. Add the dates, vanilla, cacao, and salt and blend until very smooth.

2 Transfer the mixture to a large glass jar or bowl and stir in the chia seeds. Let sit for 20 to 30 minutes, or until a gel forms. If you want a smooth and creamy pop, blend the mixture again; if you want to leave some texture, skip this step.

3 Pour the mixture into pop molds and freeze for 1 hour, then insert sticks and freeze for at least 4 hours more, or until solid.

CHOCOLATE CARAMEL SWIRL

CARAMEL

- ¾ cup full-fat coconut milk
- ¼ cup coconut sugar
- ½ teaspoon pure vanilla extract
- 1½ teaspoons coconut oil

MAKES 5 OR 6 (3-OUNCE) POPS

This might be the most decadent Glow Pop in the book. It's my go-to recipe when people say they don't like healthy desserts (although I often don't even tell people they're healthy until after they eat one—and wait for their wide eyes and dropped jaws). The secret is in the sauce—the caramel sauce, that is. Made from the simple, dairy-free combination of coconut milk, coconut sugar, coconut oil, and vanilla, this caramel is absolutely heavenly—though do keep in mind that it needs a good chill before using. It's every bit as good as the heavy cream-based caramel sauces you're used to, and I'll often use the leftovers from this recipe to drizzle over ice cream or dunk apples into when I want a sweet treat. The chocolate base is made with protein- and fiber-rich chia seeds, which lend heft and creaminess that allow the caramel to swirl through, rather than sinking straight to the bottom. These take a bit longer to freeze solid, but they're worth it!

(ingredients and recipe continue)

CHOCOLATE MIXTURE

- 1¾ cups homemade cashew milk (see page 17) or coconut milk of choice

- 5 tablespoons raw cacao powder

- ⅛ teaspoon salt

- 1 teaspoon pure vanilla extract

- 6 Medjool dates, pitted, soaked in boiling water for 10 minutes, and drained

- 5 tablespoons chia seeds

1 Make the caramel: In a small saucepan, combine the coconut milk and coconut sugar and heat over medium heat, stirring, until the sugar has dissolved. Bring just to a boil, then immediately reduce the heat to low and simmer, stirring occasionally, for 30 minutes. Remove the pot from the heat and vigorously stir in the vanilla and coconut oil. Refrigerate for at least 1 hour before using.

2 Meanwhile, make the chocolate mixture: Blend together all the ingredients for the chocolate mixture except the chia seeds until very smooth. Transfer the mixture to large jar or bowl and stir in the chia seeds. Let sit for 30 minutes, or until the mixture has thickened. Return the mixture to the blender and blend until very smooth. If necessary, add more milk 1 teaspoon at a time if you're having trouble blending.

3 Beginning with the chocolate mixture, in alternating layers, fill the molds with the chocolate mixture and caramel, one spoonful at a time. If desired, use a pop stick or knife to gently swirl the chocolate and caramel to create a marbled effect (but don't stir too much or they'll simply combine). Freeze for 1 hour, then insert sticks and freeze for at least 12 hours more, or until completely solid.

OLIVE OIL CHOCOLATE ROSEMARY

- 6 tablespoons coconut sugar
- 1⅔ cups full-fat coconut milk
- 3 sprigs fresh rosemary
- 6 tablespoons raw cacao powder
- 2 tablespoons olive oil
- Flaky sea salt, for garnish

MAKES 5 OR 6 (3-OUNCE) POPS

The chocolate and rosemary here hit your tongue first—sweet, rich, and earthy—before being grounded by the savory olive oil. The result is rich, creamy, and luxurious. This is a pop you can serve as dessert after a swanky dinner party. Afterward, you can tell your friends they consumed tons of heart-healthy fat, plenty of antioxidants, and even a bit of antiviral and antibacterial essential oils. They might thank you, or they might be too busy asking for more.

1 In a small saucepan, combine the coconut sugar and coconut milk and heat over medium heat, stirring, until the sugar has dissolved. Add the rosemary and bring to a boil, then remove from the heat. Cover and let steep for 20 minutes.

2 Remove and discard the rosemary, then transfer the mixture to a blender. Add the cacao and olive oil and blend until completely smooth.

3 Pour the mixture into pop molds. Freeze for 1 hour, then insert sticks and freeze for at least 4 hours more, or until solid. Just before serving, unmold the pops and sprinkle generously with flaky sea salt.

SAVORY

The pops in this chapter are for creative-minded people who like to play around with their food, finding surprise and delight in unexpected flavor combinations. While all these pops do have an element of sweetness, many of them contain vegetable bases, like zucchini or sweet pea, or unexpected seasonings. Some are more accessible (kids go crazy for the Cardamom Cinnamon Sweet Potato) and some are a bit more daring (I'm looking at you, Balsamic Beet & Rosemary), but all are delicious and packed with nutrients. Pops are one of my favorite places to play with flavor, since, like ice cream and doughnuts, they're the perfect vehicles for all sorts of crazy combinations.

TOMATO BEET BLOODY MARY

- 1 cup chopped peeled beet (about 1 medium beet)
- 1½ cups pure tomato juice (I like Sacramento)
- 2 garlic cloves
- Zest and juice of 1 lime
- 2 teaspoons hot sauce (or 3, if you'd like more heat)
- ¼ teaspoon celery salt
- ½ teaspoon tamari
- ⅓ cup vodka (optional)

If the smell of garlic sticks to your molds, pour a bit of distilled white vinegar into each mold after it's clean then fill them to the brim with water. Let sit for 30 minutes, then wash and rinse.

MAKES 5 OR 6 (3-OUNCE) POPS

How about a Bloody Mary that *actually* cures hangovers? Unlike the typical brunch drink, this version is loaded with vitamins and antioxidants, using real, whole-food ingredients (like—gasp!—real tomatoes) for a spicy, hearty, Sunday morning mocktail pop (or cocktail pop, if you add the vodka). This pop, based on a Bloody Mary invented by my friend Hogan, boasts a salad's worth of nutrients, but the real superstar here is beet, which, besides adding a lovely, can't-put-your-finger-on-it sweetness, is renowned for its blood- and liver-cleansing properties—exactly the parts of your body that take a beating when you drink. Garlic gets your immune system back into fighting shape, while the hot sauce kicks your metabolism into high gear to quell any day-after nausea.

1 Put the beets in a microwave-safe dish with 1 inch of water, cover, and microwave until fork-tender, 3 to 5 minutes. Alternatively, cook the beets in a stovetop steamer for 15 minutes, or until fork-tender. Let cool, then transfer to a blender, add the remaining ingredients, and blend until smooth.

2 Pour the mixture into pop molds and freeze for 1 hour, then insert sticks and freeze for at least 4 hours more, or until solid.

AVOCADO CHILE LIME

- 1 medium avocado, pitted and peeled

- ⅛ teaspoon salt

- ½ teaspoon chili powder, plus more (optional) for garnish

- Zest and juice of 1 lime

- 1 cup canned coconut milk or homemade milk of choice

- 1 tablespoon honey

MAKES 5 OR 6 (3-OUNCE) POPS

Avocado is often treated as a background ingredient: a spread to add butteriness to toast, an add-in for creaminess in a smoothie. In this pop, though, the avocado's subtly grassy, rich flavor truly shines, brought to life by a faintly acidic sweetness from the lime and a kick of umami spice from the chili powder. Avocado is a superstar for both health and beauty, prized for its good fats and antioxidants that will keep you full, quell inflammation, and make your skin absolutely glow.

1 Blend together all the ingredients until very smooth.

2 Pour the mixture into pop molds and freeze for 1 hour, then insert sticks and freeze for at least 4 hours more, or until solid. Just before serving, unmold the pops and sprinkle each with chili powder, if desired.

ZUCCHINI BASIL

- 1¾ cups coarsely chopped zucchini

- ¾ cup packed fresh basil leaves

- 3 tablespoons honey

- ¾ cup full-fat coconut or almond milk

- 2 tablespoons fresh lemon juice

MAKES 5 OR 6 (3-OUNCE) POPS

This pop is inspired by one of my favorite soups, created by famed Chicago chef Grant Achatz of Michelin-starred Alinea. I love how delicate it is; basil is a beautifully sweet, tender herb, and zucchini makes a wonderfully creamy base for its flavor to shine. The acid from the lemon and just a touch of honey bring the whole thing to life. Zucchini is one of my favorite vegetables. It is packed with vitamin C and bone-building manganese, and is rich in fiber and incredibly filling. This is one of my favorite pops to eat when I'm feeling peckish, as the flavor is interesting enough to stave off boredom (which, to be honest, is one of the main reasons I often find myself eating) and satiating enough to eliminate my hunger for hours.

1   Put the zucchini in a microwave-safe dish with 1 inch of water, cover, and microwave until fork-tender, 2 to 4 minutes. Alternatively, cook the zucchini in a stovetop steamer for 10 to 15 minutes, or until fork-tender. Let cool until warm to the touch, then transfer to a blender, add the remaining ingredients, and blend until smooth.

2   Pour the mixture into pop molds and freeze for 1 hour, then insert sticks and freeze for at least 4 hours more, or until solid.

CURRIED BUTTERNUT SQUASH

- 3 cups coarsely chopped peeled butternut squash (about 1 medium butternut squash)

- 2 teaspoons curry powder

- ⅛ teaspoon salt

- 2 tablespoons maple syrup

- ¼ cup coconut milk of choice

MAKES 5 OR 6 (3-OUNCE) POPS

This pop is like an exotic vacation for your tongue. Curry, a staple in Indian cuisine, brings to life sweet, lightly steamed butternut squash. Although you buy it as a single spice, curry powder refers to a blend that varies by region and producer, but typically includes turmeric, coriander, cumin, fenugreek, and chile peppers. Lightly spicy and richly earthy, it packs a flavor and nutritional punch, with myriad antiaging and anti-inflammatory benefits from its many components. Feel free to buy ready-made curry or make your own, playing around with the various spices until you've found the perfect flavor to suit your taste buds. Either way, this pop will surprise and delight!

1 Put the squash in a microwave-safe dish with 1 inch of water, cover, and microwave until very soft, 2 to 4 minutes. Alternatively, cook the squash in a stovetop steamer for 10 to15 minutes, or until very soft. Let cool until warm to the touch, then transfer to a blender, add the remaining ingredients, and blend until smooth.

2 Pour the mixture into pop molds and freeze for 1 hour, then insert sticks and freeze for at least 4 hours more, or until solid.

SWEET-&-SPICY CORN

- 1½ cups fresh or frozen corn kernels
- 1 cup full-fat coconut milk
- 3 tablespoons coconut sugar
- 1 serrano chile, halved lengthwise, stemmed, and seeded
- Zest and juice of 1 lime
- Chili powder, for garnish (optional)

MAKES 5 OR 6 (3-OUNCE) POPS

In this pop, the sweetness of the corn plays off the spiciness of the serrano chile, and the lime adds a zesty brightness. Chili powder, isn't actually that spicy, but it adds a beautiful savory flavor here. Different peppers have unique flavors and health benefits, which range from boosting metabolism to boosting immunity. Several politicians are rumored to eat a pepper a day to avoid getting sick on the mega-germ-filled campaign trail!

1   In a medium pot, bring 3 cups water to a boil over high heat. Add the corn and boil for 2 minutes (if fresh) or 3 minutes (if frozen). Drain, then submerge in ice water to stop the cooking.

2   In the now empty pot, combine the coconut milk, coconut sugar, and chile and bring just to a simmer over medium-low heat. Reduce the heat to low and cook, stirring occasionally, for 15 minutes. Remove from the heat and let cool for 10 minutes, then remove and discard the chile.

3   Transfer the milk mixture to a blender. Drain the corn and add it to the milk mixture along with the lime zest and juice. Blend until smooth.

4   Pour the mixture into pop molds and freeze for 1 hour, then insert sticks and freeze for at least 4 hours more, or until solid. Just before serving, unmold the pops and sprinkle each with chili powder, if desired.

BALSAMIC BEET & ROSEMARY

- 3 cups coarsely chopped peeled beets (2 or 3 beets)

- 2 tablespoons coconut oil, melted

- ⅛ teaspoon salt

- 1 cup balsamic vinegar

- 2 sprigs fresh rosemary

- 2 cups water

- 2 tablespoons honey

MAKES 5 OR 6 (3-OUNCE) POPS

This pop always feels so sophisticated to me, the equivalent of a swanky cocktail party on a stick (although the sweetness, and, to be frank, its messiness, are quite appealing to children as well). Beets are often relegated to salads, but they have a wonderfully complex, mildly sweet flavor that works well in everything from root vegetable mash to soups to this very pop. The trick is to roast them: this dulls the "dirty" flavor that beet-haters often react to, and causes the outsides to become beautifully caramelized. Paired with a rosemary balsamic reduction that swirls throughout the pop, the beet is elevated with every bite from humble salad accoutrement to the main star—and oh, what a star it is. Beets get their gorgeous pigment from betalains, a potent and somewhat rare class of antioxidants that have been linked to the support of nervous system health and the prevention and treatment of a number of cancers.

(recipe continues)

1 Preheat the oven to 375°F. Toss the beets with the coconut oil and salt, then arrange them in an even layer on a parchment paper–lined baking sheet. Roast for 40 to 50 minutes, or until fork-tender.

2 Meanwhile, in a small saucepan, combine the balsamic vinegar and rosemary and bring just to a simmer over medium-high heat; then reduce the heat to low and simmer, stirring occasionally, until the mixture reduces by half and has a thick, syrupy consistency. Remove from the heat and set aside.

3 Let the beets cool until warm to the touch, then transfer to a blender. Add the water and honey and blend until very smooth.

4 In alternating layers, fill the molds with the beet mixture and balsamic syrup (it's okay if they swirl together—you're looking for a marbled effect). Freeze for 1 hour, then insert sticks and freeze for at least 4 hours more, or until solid.

SWEET PEA & MINT

- 1½ cups fresh or frozen peas
- ¾ cup packed fresh mint leaves
- 3 tablespoons honey
- ¾ cup full-fat coconut milk
- 2 tablespoons fresh lemon juice

MAKES 5 OR 6 (3-OUNCE) POPS

Mint and peas go together like, well, two peas in a pod; the mint is incredibly refreshing, balancing and elevating the starchy sweetness of the peas. Peas also offer a ton of health benefits (good to hear, I'm sure, as your mother was likely always making you finish yours). Besides being rich in vitamin K, manganese, fiber, and B vitamins (including folate, which is great for pregnant women), they're also one of the few dietary sources of pisumsaponins I and II and pisumosides A and B, phytonutrients that have been found to help combat type 2 diabetes. Studies also indicate that eating a serving or two of peas daily helps reduce the risk of stomach cancer. While fresh peas do taste minutely brighter, the difference is slight enough that I'll often reach for frozen.

1 In a medium pot, bring 3 cups water to a boil over high heat. Add the peas and cook for 2 minutes (if fresh) or 3 minutes (if frozen). Drain and submerge in ice water, then drain again.

2 Transfer the peas to a blender. Add the remaining ingredients and blend until smooth.

3 Pour the mixture into pop molds and freeze for 1 hour, then insert sticks and freeze for at least 4 hours more, or until solid.

CARDAMOM CINNAMON SWEET POTATO

- 1 large sweet potato
- ¾ cup canned coconut milk or homemade milk of choice
- 1 teaspoon ground cinnamon
- ½ teaspoon ground cardamom
- 4 Medjool dates, pitted, soaked in boiling water for 10 minutes, and drained
- 1 teaspoon pure vanilla extract

MAKES 5 OR 6 (3-OUNCE) POPS

Kids go nuts for these sweet and creamy pops. Cardamom has a citrusy, spicy-sweet flavor, and is commonly found in Middle Eastern and Scandinavian cooking in both savory dishes and desserts. While it's packed with vitamins and minerals, particularly iron, potassium, and manganese (one teaspoon contains 150 percent of your daily requirement), many of its health benefits are thanks to its essential volatile oils, which work in the body in a more potent, medicinal way. Recent studies have shown that consumption of cardamom reduces the incidence of colorectal cancer, and helps to treat it as well. It also controls hypertension, lowers cholesterol, and aids in digestion. Sweet potatoes are no health slouch either, with each of these pops boasting 100 percent of your recommended daily vitamin A, a potent antioxidant that boosts your immune system and helps with eye health. The only sugar in this recipe comes from the fiber-packed sweet potatoes and dates, making it a great light breakfast or hearty snack.

Roasting a sweet potato helps caramelize its sugars and bring out its innate sweetness. My approach, described below, is super simple—I don't even wash the sweet potato first, as I'll be discarding the skin. I love to eat leftover sweet potato mash with a pat of butter or ghee, a dash of vanilla, and a generous shake of cinnamon—it tastes like pumpkin pie and is a great, filling snack.

1 Preheat the oven to 400°F. Place the sweet potato on a parchment paper–lined baking sheet and roast for 45 to 60 minutes, or until very soft. Remove and let cool completely.

2 Halve the sweet potato and scoop the flesh into a blender, discarding the skin. Add the remaining ingredients and blend until very smooth

3 Pour the mixture into pop molds and freeze for 1 hour, then insert sticks and freeze for at least 4 hours more, or until solid.

PUMPKIN PIE

- ¾ cup canned coconut milk or homemade milk of choice
- 1 cup fresh or canned pumpkin puree (see Tip)
- 5 Medjool dates, pitted, soaked in boiling water for 10 minutes, and drained
- 1 teaspoon pure vanilla extract
- ¾ teaspoon ground cinnamon
- ½ teaspoon ground ginger
- ½ teaspoon freshly grated nutmeg
- ¼ teaspoon ground allspice
- ⅛ teaspoon ground cloves
- ⅛ teaspoon salt

MAKES 5 OR 6 (3-OUNCE) POPS

This pop makes pumpkin pie flavor accessible anytime. Pumpkins are rich in vitamin A—one serving contains more than 200 percent of your recommended daily intake. Vitamin A is important for both skin and eye health, and should be consumed with fat (such as coconut milk) to be absorbed properly. Pumpkins are also rich in potassium, and their fiber will keep you full while helping to cleanse your intestinal tract. Their beta-carotene has been found to reduce bodily inflammation, and protect against heart disease, lung cancer, and skin cancer. Mixed together with the health benefits of the spices, this pop packs quite a health punch.

1 Blend together all the ingredients until very smooth.

2 Pour the mixture into pop molds and freeze for 1 hour, then insert sticks and freeze for at least 4 hours more, or until solid.

To make your own pumpkin puree, scoop out a 4- to 6-pound pumpkin, brush with neutral oil, and sprinkle with sea salt. Bake cut-side down on a parchment–lined baking sheet at 400°F. Let cool, then scrape out the flesh and puree until smooth. You should have 2 to 3 cups pumpkin puree. Store in an airtight container in the fridge for up to 1 week or in the freezer for up to 5 months.

THAI PEANUT CILANTRO GINGER

- 1 cup coconut milk of choice
- 3 tablespoons honey
- ¼ cup unsalted peanut butter (creamy and crunchy both work well)
- ¼ cup packed fresh cilantro leaves
- Zest and juice of 1 lime
- 1 (1-inch) piece fresh ginger, peeled and grated
- ¼ teaspoon salt (omit if using salted peanut butter)
- ¼ cup roasted salted peanuts

MAKES 5 OR 6 (3-OUNCE) POPS

Based on the sauce used in a traditional Thai satay, this peanut-buttery pop is hearty enough for a light meal and packed with good-for-you ingredients. The cilantro, in addition to adding a citrusy, herby zip, is one of nature's best chelators, renowned for clearing the body of chemicals and heavy metals (accumulated from the environment). Peanuts, which are not actually nuts at all, but rather legumes, are rich in monounsaturated fatty acids like oleic acid, which helps to lower LDL (or "bad") cholesterol and increase HDL (or "good") cholesterol in the blood. The ginger, honey, and coconut milk help these pops straddle the sweet and savory line, while also adding further antibacterial benefits.

1   Blend together all the ingredients except the roasted peanuts until very smooth. Add the peanuts and pulse until well distributed but not completely blended.

2   Pour the mixture into pop molds and freeze for 1 hour, then insert sticks and freeze for at least 4 hours more, or until solid.

ROASTED CARROT THYME

- 1 cup coarsely chopped carrots
- 1 teaspoon melted coconut oil
- ⅛ teaspoon salt
- 1 cup canned coconut milk or homemade milk of choice
- 2 tablespoons maple syrup
- 1 teaspoon fresh thyme leaves

MAKES 5 OR 6 (3-OUNCE) POPS

This pop is rich enough to be a light meal, but sweet enough to be a real treat. The health benefits of carrots multiply substantially when the vegetable is cooked; plus, roasting them caramelizes their sugars. One of these pops contains more than 100 percent of the recommended daily amount of vitamin A, as well as a host of other vitamins and minerals. Thyme adds a subtle, herbaceous sweetness, but it's also powerfully antibacterial, even in very small doses, making this a wonderful choice to fight off—or prevent—colds.

1 Preheat the oven to 400°F. Toss the carrots with the coconut oil and salt and arrange them in a single layer on a parchment paper–lined baking sheet. Transfer to the oven and roast for 45 minutes, or until the edges are browned. Remove and let cool for 15 to 20 minutes, until cool to the touch.

2 Transfer the carrots to a blender and add the milk and maple syrup. Blend until very smooth. Add the thyme and pulse until the pieces are small and well distributed but still visible.

3 Pour the mixture into pop molds and freeze for 1 hour, then insert sticks and freeze for at least 4 hours more, or until solid.

GREEN

The pops in this chapter put health at the absolute forefront. While the others forgo simple sugars for mineral-rich honey, maple syrup, or coconut syrup, the pops in this section are 100 percent sweetener-free, deriving their sweetness only from fruits like bananas, dates (see page 21), mangoes, and strawberries. Each pop also contains a complete serving of vegetables in the form of leafy greens, which are some of nature's healthiest foods. They are packed with fiber, chlorophyll (which serves as a cell builder), and tons of vitamins and nutrients, detailed in each recipe. These health benefits don't come at the expense of flavor, however. The pops are designed to either highlight the flavor of the greens (in the case of basil and cilantro, they'll knock your socks off), or completely mask them (you'd never know there was more than a cup of spinach packed into the Chocolate-Covered Strawberry pops). They're great for children who might turn their nose up at a salad, but will always say yes to a Mint Chocolate Chip pop.

STRAWBERRY SPINACH BASIL

- ½ cup packed fresh basil leaves

- ½ cup packed spinach

- ⅔ cup homemade almond or cashew milk (see page 17)

- 1½ cups hulled fresh or frozen strawberries

- 2 Medjool dates, pitted, soaked in boiling water for 10 minutes, and drained

MAKES 5 OR 6 (3-OUNCE) POPS

Basil is one of my favorite herbs to use in desserts, as it has a lovely sweetness that's brought to life when paired with the naturally occurring sugars found in fruits. Strawberry, in my opinion, is its soulmate: together, they're sweet and just a bit savory, which adds a wonderful depth to the resulting pop. The health benefits of basil come from its flavonoids—which have been found to be cell protective—and volatile oils, which contain estragole, linalool, cineole, eugenol, sabinene, myrcene, and limonene. These oils are strongly antibacterial (this pop is, in fact, great to eat if you're recovering from any type of food poisoning), as well as anti-inflammatory, working the same way in the body as over-the-counter NSAIDs. So, the next time you feel a headache coming on, reach for this pop instead of the medicine cabinet—your body and your taste buds will thank you!

1   Blend together the basil, spinach, and milk until smooth. Add the strawberries and dates and blend again until very smooth.

2   Pour the mixture into pop molds and freeze for 1 hour, then insert sticks and freeze for at least 4 hours more, or until solid.

SPICY ARUGULA JALAPEÑO PINEAPPLE

- Zest and juice of 1 lime

- ½ banana

- 1 cup arugula

- 1 cup fresh or frozen cubed pineapple

- 1 jalapeño, stemmed, seeded, and deveined

- ¾ cup coconut water

- ⅛ teaspoon salt

- ½ teaspoon pure vanilla extract

MAKES 5 OR 6 (3-OUNCE) POPS

Attention, spicy food fans: This pop is for you. A play on a salsa from one of my favorite Mexican restaurants, this pop is a sweet and spicy dream. The pineapple cuts through the fiery jalapeño, and the arugula, which has a peppery, earthy flavor, acts as a spicy complement. These are amazing if you feel yourself coming down with a cold, as one jalapeño contains 18 percent of the recommended daily vitamin C, and its spiciness can help clear mucus from your nose and throat. Like all hot peppers, jalapeños contain capsaicin, which has been shown to help with weight loss, especially in the stubborn belly fat area, in addition to offering protection from cancer and heart disease. Be careful to remove the seeds and all the white membrane from your pepper before blending, though, or your tongue might get a bit more heat than it's ready for!

1   Blend together all the ingredients until very smooth.

2   Pour the mixture into pop molds and freeze for 1 hour, then insert sticks and freeze for at least 4 hours more, or until solid.

TURMERIC MANGO SUNRISE

- 1½ cups lightly packed spinach

- ¾ cup canned coconut milk or homemade milk of choice

- 1½ cups fresh or frozen mango

- 1 teaspoon ground turmeric

- ⅛ teaspoon freshly ground black pepper

- ⅛ teaspoon salt

- 1 teaspoon pure vanilla extract

- Zest and juice of 1 orange

MAKES 5 OR 6 (3-OUNCE) POPS

This green smoothie pop is all about getting that glowing skin. Turmeric, one of my absolute favorite superfoods, quells any inflammation in your body, while mango is rich in vitamins A and C. These are *the* vitamins to look for in topical skin care (retinol, which is derived from vitamin A, is considered the holy grail of antiaging products), and they work similarly inside your body, helping to build collagen, which keeps your skin plump and youthful. I love using citrus zest in summery pops: besides adding a wonderful, lively flavor (these pops taste like a sunny day), they help protect against the type of cell damage that causes skin cancer. So go ahead—grab your sunscreen and your Turmeric Mango Sunrise Glow Pop, and head out to catch some of those luscious rays!

1 Blend together the spinach and milk until smooth. Add the remaining ingredients and blend until very smooth.

2 Pour the mixture into pop molds and freeze for 1 hour, then insert sticks and freeze for at least 4 hours more, or until solid.

MANGO ARUGULA CILANTRO

- ½ cup packed arugula

- ½ cup packed fresh cilantro, woody ends removed (see Tip)

- 1 cup canned coconut milk or homemade milk of choice

- 1½ cups coarsely chopped fresh or frozen mango

- ½ banana

- 3 Medjool dates, pitted, soaked in boiling water for 10 minutes, and drained

When blending cilantro for pops, feel free to leave most of the stem after discarding the woody ends—the stems contain much of the flavor!

MAKES 5 OR 6 (3-OUNCE) POPS

While it's often relegated to the role of garnish, I like to use cilantro as a star ingredient. I love its fresh, green flavor and citrusy bite. Combined with arugula's spicy, peppery notes and mellowed by mango's creamy sweetness, this pop is like a beach vacation in your mouth. It's great to include cilantro as a regular part of your diet, because it's one of the best natural chelators, which means that it cleans your blood, ridding it of heavy metal buildup and other toxins we accumulate naturally as part of our modern lifestyles. This is one of my favorite pops to eat after a weekend spent engaging in a bit of debauchery, whether it's eating poorly, drinking too much, or simply not taking care of myself, as it cleans out my system and readies me to start fresh.

1 Blend together the arugula, cilantro, and milk until smooth. Add the remaining ingredients and blend until very smooth.

2 Pour the mixture into pop molds and freeze for 1 hour, then insert sticks and freeze for at least 4 hours more, or until solid.

CINNAMON BERRY

- 1½ cups lightly packed kale leaves
- 1⅓ cups canned coconut milk or homemade milk of choice
- 2 cups fresh or frozen mixed berries
- ½ banana
- 2 teaspoons ground cinnamon
- ⅛ teaspoon sea salt

MAKES 5 OR 6 (3-OUNCE) POPS

This is a pop version of my own personal go-to green smoothie. There are no fancy superfoods or exotic fruits in it, which means I usually have everything on hand. The creamy milk and warm, earthy cinnamon highlight the sweetness in all berries, so you can really play around based on your taste preferences: I like to use a mix of blackberries, raspberries, and blueberries, which are all antiaging, fiber-packed powerhouses, and incredibly delicious. This recipe also includes kale, a leafy green that's gotten quite a lot of press in the last few years. Despite being too trendy for its own good, kale is an amazing choice to include in green pops: a cruciferous vegetable, it supports your body's own detoxification processes.

1 Blend together the kale and milk until smooth. Add the remaining ingredients and blend until very smooth.

2 Pour the mixture into pop molds and freeze for 1 hour, then insert sticks and freeze for at least 4 hours more, or until solid.

MINT CHOCOLATE CHIP

- ½ cup packed fresh mint leaves
- ½ cup packed spinach
- ¾ cup homemade cashew milk (see page 17)
- 2 bananas
- ½ teaspoon peppermint extract (optional; see Tip)
- ½ teaspoon pure vanilla extract
- ⅛ teaspoon sea salt
- ¼ cup raw cacao nibs or dark chocolate chips

MAKES 5 OR 6 (3-OUNCE) POPS

In every bite of this pop, the silky texture gives way to crunchy bits of cacao that explode into chocolate goodness. This pop gets its flavor from two types of mint: fresh leaves and peppermint extract. Both are incredibly soothing to your stomach (and to your mind as well: on a hot day, a few bites of mint are like an icy gust of fresh air for your insides). Cacao nibs are, essentially, chocolate in its purest form, created by simply roasting and then crushing the beans. They're incredibly dense in the antioxidants and minerals that chocolate is known for. Because you can't taste the spinach in these at all, they're fun pops to give to people who think they don't like "health food," and kids absolutely go wild for them. Be sure to use only the mint leaves, as the stems are very bitter.

While the peppermint extract will add a stronger, more multilayered mint flavor, these pops are absolutely delicious without it, so feel free to omit it if you don't have it on hand.

1 Blend together the mint, spinach, and milk until smooth. Add the bananas, peppermint extract (if using), vanilla, and salt and blend until very smooth. Add the cacao nibs and pulse just until well distributed but still intact.

2 Pour the mixture into pop molds and freeze for 1 hour, then insert sticks and freeze for at least 4 hours more, or until solid.

LEMON GINGER

- 2 cups lightly packed spinach

- 1 cup coconut milk of choice

- Zest and juice of 2 lemons

- 1 ripe banana

- 1 (1-inch) piece fresh ginger, peeled and grated

MAKES 5 OR 6 (3-OUNCE) POPS

Ginger is one of my favorite flavors to pair with lemon; I'll often make a ginger-lemon tea when I'm feeling under the weather, and ginger lemonade is a summer staple for me. There's a reason the combination feels so good when you're sick: ginger is one of the most powerful anti-inflammatory foods around. It quells nausea and indigestion and helps with arthritis, post-workout pain, and other inflammation-related conditions, while lemons offer a powerful dose of immunity-boosting vitamin C. This pop utilizes the nutrient- and flavor-rich zest of the lemon, but be sure to avoid the white membrane underneath the bright-yellow, citrus oil–packed exterior, as it's incredibly bitter. I like to use mild-tasting spinach in this pop to really let the ginger and lemon shine, while still getting all the benefits of the leafy green's digestion-boosting fiber and skin-loving vitamins C and K.

1 Blend together the spinach and milk until smooth. Add the remaining ingredients and blend until very smooth.

2 Pour the mixture into pop molds and freeze for 1 hour, then insert sticks and freeze for at least 4 hours more, or until solid.

CHOCOLATE-COVERED STRAWBERRY

- 1½ cups lightly packed spinach

- 1 cup canned coconut milk or homemade milk of choice

- 1½ cups hulled fresh or frozen strawberries

- 5 tablespoons raw cacao powder

- ½ banana

- ⅛ teaspoon salt

- 1 teaspoon pure vanilla extract

- 3 Medjool dates, pitted, soaked in boiling water for 10 minutes, and drained

MAKES 5 OR 6 (3-OUNCE) POPS

Chocolate-covered strawberries might be my favorite dessert. The rich, velvety chocolate so perfectly sets off the delicate, fruity sweetness of the berries. Raw cacao, prized by the Aztecs as the bean of the gods, is one of the highest known natural sources of magnesium, copper, zinc, iron, chromium, and manganese—all minerals in which many people are deficient. In addition, raw cacao contains a unique alkaloid chemical called theobromine, a known mood booster, and provides a mild stimulatory effect without the buzzy feeling of caffeine. Spinach is the perfect fiber-rich base for this pop, as its mild flavor lets the decadent strawberry-chocolate goodness shine through.

1   Blend together the spinach and milk until smooth. Add the remaining ingredients and blend until very smooth.

2   Pour the mixture into pop molds and freeze for 1 hour, then insert sticks and freeze for at least 4 hours more, or until solid.

THE ULTIMATE GREEN SMOOTHIE

- 1 cup lightly packed mixed greens, like romaine, kale, and spinach
- 1 cup canned coconut milk or homemade milk of choice
- 1 ripe banana
- 1 medium apple, cored and cut into cubes
- ⅛ teaspoon sea salt

I prefer to use Granny Smith apples in this smoothie, due to their low sugar content and tart, delicious flavor, but any type of apple will work well.

MAKES 5 OR 6 (3-OUNCE) POPS

If you've ever bought a bottled green juice at your local juice bar or grocery store, you'll have a good idea of what this pop tastes like. That classic smoothie gets quite a bit of its flavor from apple, with the greens brightening and freshening the overall taste. I love this one for breakfast or as an afternoon pick-me-up. The greens bulk it out with fiber to keep you full and satiated, while the apple and banana give sweetness to add extra bounce to your day. This is a great green smoothie pop to get started with, as you likely have most—if not all—of the ingredients in your kitchen right now!

1 Blend together the greens and milk until smooth. Add the remaining ingredients and blend until very smooth.

2 Pour the mixture into pop molds and freeze for 1 hour, then insert sticks and freeze for at least 4 hours more, or until solid.

DOUBLE CHOCOLATE BROWNIE

- 1 cup lightly packed spinach

- 1⅓ cups canned coconut milk or homemade milk of choice

- 5 tablespoons raw cacao powder

- 2 bananas

- ½ avocado

- ⅛ teaspoon salt

- 1 teaspoon pure vanilla extract

- 3 Medjool dates, pitted, soaked in boiling water for 10 minutes, and drained

- 3 tablespoons cacao nibs

MAKES 5 OR 6 (3-OUNCE) POPS

If you're one of those people who likes your chocolate with a side of chocolate, this pop is for you. The greens-filled base is like a healthy frozen brownie batter. You know all those studies about chocolate's health benefits? Raw cacao is the kind they're talking about, as many of the vitamins and minerals are lost during roasting and processing. This pop contains cacao in two forms: the powder is blended with creamy, sweet bananas and dates to make a brownie batter base, which is then studded with crunchy cacao nibs. The avocado and spinach (the flavors of which are overpowered completely by all that chocolate deliciousness) add enough good fat and fiber to make this an awesome breakfast—filling enough to keep you going through lunch, and tasty enough to make you feel like you're sneaking in a decadent dessert.

1 Blend together the spinach and milk until smooth. Add the remaining ingredients except the cacao nibs and blend until very smooth. Add the cacao nibs and pulse until well distributed but still intact.

2 Pour the mixture into pop molds and freeze for 1 hour, then insert sticks and freeze for at least 4 hours more, or until solid.

PIÑA COLADA

- 1½ cups lightly packed spinach
- 1 cup coconut milk of choice
- 1½ cups cubed fresh or frozen pineapple
- ½ banana
- ⅛ teaspoon salt
- 1 teaspoon pure vanilla extract
- 3 tablespoons unsweetened flaked coconut (optional)

MAKES 5 OR 6 (3-OUNCE) POPS

Is there any drink that screams fun more than a piña colada? A virgin version of the tropical cocktail works perfectly as a green smoothie pop: the sweet pineapple and creamy coconut beautifully mask the flavor of the spinach (a neutral mixed green blend would also work well here). Pineapple is the only food source of an enzyme called bromelain, which helps you digest and maximize nutrient absorption from your food—and it's so potent that it's often sold in supplement form. Am I saying you should start every meal with a piña colada Glow Pop? Well . . . let's just say I'm not saying you *shouldn't*.

1 Blend together the spinach and milk until smooth. Add the remaining ingredients except the coconut flakes and blend until very smooth.

2 Pour the mixture into pop molds and sprinkle with the coconut flakes, if desired. Freeze for 1 hour, then insert sticks and freeze for at least 4 hours more, or until solid.

APPENDIX

	CANCER FIGHTING	HEART HEALTHY	BRAIN BOOSTING	BLOAT REDUCING	GOOD FOR THE GUT	DETOXIFYING
Apple Pie, p. 29	*	*				
Cucumber Mint Mojito, p. 31				*		
Watermelon Lime, p.32		*		*	*	
Chamomile Cantaloupe Mint, p. 35				*	*	*
Mango Chile, p. 36	*	*	*			*
Rosemary Strawberry, p. 37	*	*				
Honeyed Peach Thyme, p. 38	*					
Pink Lemonade, p. 41		*		*	*	*
Lavender Blueberry, p. 42	*	*	*	*	*	*
Blackberry Rose, p. 44	*					
Caramelized Pineapple, p. 45				*	*	*
Coconut Chai, p. 49	*					*
Cinnamon Orange & Cream, p. 50	*				*	
Strawberry Cardamom Rose Lassi, p. 51				*	*	
Mexican Horchata, p. 52		*				
Cookie Dough, p. 53	*					
Blueberry & Cream, p. 55	*		*			
Matcha Latte, p. 56	*	*	*			
Turmeric Golden Milk, p. 59	*		*			*
Peanut Butter & Jelly, p. 60					*	
Lavender London Fog, p. 63	*	*				
White Chocolate Chia Strawberry, p. 65		*			*	
Mexican Hot Chocolate, p. 69	*					
Chocolate Fudge, p. 70	*				*	
Chocolate-Covered Banana, p. 71	*	*		*		
Chocolate Hazelnut, p. 75	*	*				

PROMOTES WEIGHT LOSS	GLOWING SKIN	CALMING	ENERGIZING	MEAL REPLACING	PAIN RELIEVING	ALLERGY RELIEVING	IMMUNE BOOSTING	HYDRATING
*							*	
	*							*
	*				*		*	*
*	*	*						*
*	*		*		*		*	
	*						*	
						*	*	
	*							*
	*	*					*	*
	*	*					*	
								*
*			*		*	*	*	
*	*		*				*	
*	*	*						
*								
	*							
							*	
			*				*	
	*		*		*	*	*	
				*				*
		*	*					
			*	*				
			*		*		*	
	*	*	*	*				
	*		*					
	*		*					

	CANCER FIGHTING	HEART HEALTHY	BRAIN BOOSTING	BLOAT REDUCING	GOOD FOR THE GUT	DETOXIFYING
Cold-Brew Mocha, p. 76	*	*	*			
Neapolitan, p. 78		*		*	*	
Chocolate Orange, p. 81	*	*	*			
Peanut Butter Cup, p. 82						
Chocolate Chia Lavender, p. 84	*				*	
Chocolate Caramel Swirl, p. 85					*	
Olive Oil Chocolate Rosemary, p. 88	*	*	*			*
Tomato Beet Bloody Mary, p. 93	*	*			*	*
Avocado Chile Lime, p. 95	*	*	*	*	*	*
Zucchini Basil, p. 96						
Curried Butternut Squash, p. 97	*	*			*	*
Sweet-&-Spicy Corn, p. 98						
Balsamic Beet & Rosemary, p. 101	*	*	*			
Sweet Pea & Mint, p. 103				*	*	
Cardamom Cinnamon Sweet Potato, p. 104	*	*			*	*
Pumpkin Pie, p. 106	*	*	*	*	*	
Thai Peanut Cilantro Ginger, p. 107		*			*	*
Roasted Carrot Thyme, p. 109	*					
Strawberry Spinach Basil, p. 113	*		*	*	*	*
Spicy Arugula Jalapeño Pineapple, p. 115	*	*		*	*	*
Turmeric Mango Sunrise, p. 116	*	*	*	*	*	*
Mango Arugula Cilantro, p. 118	*	*	*	*	*	*
Cinnamon Berry, p. 119	*		*	*	*	*
Mint Chocolate Chip, p. 121	*			*	*	*
Lemon Ginger, p. 122	*			*	*	*
Chocolate-Covered Strawberry, p. 123	*		*		*	
The Ultimate Green Smoothie, p. 124	*	*	*	*	*	*
Double Chocolate Brownie, p. 126	*	*	*	*	*	
Piña Colada, p. 127	*			*	*	*

PROMOTES WEIGHT LOSS	GLOWING SKIN	CALMING	ENERGIZING	MEAL REPLACING	PAIN RELIEVING	ALLERGY RELIEVING	IMMUNE BOOSTING	HYDRATING
			*					
*	*		*	*			*	*
	*	*	*					
	*			*				
			*	*				
			*	*				
	*			*		*	*	
					*		*	*
*	*			*				*
				*		*		
*	*			*	*	*	*	
*					*		*	
				*		*		
*	*			*			*	
*	*			*	*		*	
				*			*	
	*					*		
*	*			*	*		*	*
*	*				*		*	*
*	*			*	*	*	*	
*	*			*			*	
*	*			*	*		*	*
*	*	*		*	*		*	*
*	*	*		*	*	*		*
*	*	*	*	*			*	
*	*			*			*	*
*	*	*	*	*			*	
*	*			*	*		*	*

GLOW GLOSSARY

Almonds: Almonds are rich in skin-smoothing vitamin E, bone-building and heart-supporting calcium, and biotin, which is great for your hair, skin, and nails. They're also packed with protein and heart-healthy fats.

Apples: Apple contain quercetin, a potent antioxidant that may help protect against heart disease and cancer, in addition to having antihistamine and anti-inflammatory effects. They also boast a ton of soluble fiber, which helps cleanse your intestines and leaves you feeling slim and detoxified.

Arugula: Arugula contains high levels of blood-pressure-lowering nitrates, along with sulfuric compounds that have been found to lower the risk of many types of cancer. Like all leafy greens, it's rich in cleansing, filling fiber and vitamin K.

Avocado: Avocado is a superstar for both health and beauty, prized for its good fats and antioxidants that will keep you full, quell inflammation, and make your skin absolutely glow.

Bananas: Bananas are rich in potassium, fiber, and skin-brightening vitamin C, which boosts both youth-enriching collagen and general immunity.

Basil: The benefits of basil come from its flavonoids—which have been found to be cell-protective—and volatile oils, including estragole, linalool, cineole, eugenol, sabinene, myrcene, and limonene. These oils are strongly antibacterial as well as anti-inflammatory, and work the same way in the body as over-the-counter NSAIDs.

Beet: Beets get their pigment from betalains, a potent and somewhat rare class of antioxidants that has been linked to supporting nervous system health and prevention and treatment of a number of cancers. They're also high in immune-boosting vitamin C and, if consumed before exercising, have been found to enhance both energy and stamina.

Black Pepper: Black pepper contains piperine, a compound that dramatically increases the body's absorption of other nutrients.

Black Tea: Black tea contains two types of antioxidants, catechins and polyphenols, which have been found to ward off certain types of cancer, reduce the risk of stroke and type 2 diabetes, and defend against heart disease.

Blackberry: Just one serving of blackberries has more than a third of your daily dose of vitamin C, and both soluble and insoluble fiber, which clean out your intestines. These are also rich in phytochemicals that protect against cancer, aging, and inflammation.

Blueberry: Blueberries have the highest antioxidant capacity of any commonly consumed fruit or vegetable, resulting in protection against heart disease and cell damage. They're also shown to help increase memory function and prevent cognitive decline, and their compounds are being studied as a potential Alzheimer's treatment. Similar to cranberries, they're also effective in preventing and fighting UTIs.

Butternut Squash: Butternut squash gets its color from carotenoids, the same powerful antioxidants found in carrots and sweet potatoes that help enhance eye health and protect against heart disease. One cup of butternut squash contains half your daily recommended intake of vitamin C, which is wonderful for both glowing skin and boosting the immune system. It's also rich in fiber, potassium, and vitamin B6.

Cacao (Nibs and Powder): Cacao is one of the greatest known natural sources of magnesium, copper, zinc, iron, chromium, and manganese—all minerals that many people are deficient in. In addition, raw cacao contains a unique alkaloid chemical called theobromine, which provides a mild stimulatory effect without the buzzy feeling of caffeine.

Cacao Butter, Raw: Cacao butter is the pressed oil of the cacao bean. Like cacao powder and nibs, cacao butter is rich in antioxidants; oleic acid, which has been shown to reduce the risk of heart disease; and theobromine, which raises energy and alertness levels.

Cantaloupe: One cup of cantaloupe has 75 percent of your recommended daily intake of vitamin C, which helps build skin collagen and boost immunity. It's also rich in vitamin A and potassium, and, like all melons, is incredibly hydrating.

Cardamom: While it's packed with vitamins and minerals—particularly iron, potassium, and manganese (one teaspoon contains 150 percent of your daily requirement)—many of cardamom's health benefits come from its essential volatile oils, which work in the body in a more potent, medicinal way. Recent studies have shown that consumption of cardamom reduces incidents of colorectal cancer and helps to treat it as well. It also controls hypertension, lowers cholesterol, and aids in digestion.

Cashews: Cashews contain high levels of lutein and zeaxanthin, antioxidants that particularly benefit eye health. They also contain arginine, an amino acid that helps with heart health, and have been shown in studies to reduce the risk of type 2 diabetes.

Cayenne: Cayenne breaks up mucus, making it ideal to consume when you have a cold or the flu, and it speeds up your metabolism. It also turns on your body's natural pain management system—so the next time you hurt yourself, eat some cayenne instead of popping a pain killer!

Chamomile: Chamomile tea is made from dried chamomile flower buds. It's caffeine-free and known for calming each and every part of your body, from muscle spasms and menstrual cramps to insomnia and anxiety.

Chile Peppers: Chile peppers contain capsaicin, a potent anti-inflammatory and metabolism-boosting compound. They've been shown to reduce LDL ("bad") cholesterol and lower the risk of strokes and heart attacks.

Cilantro: While cilantro is rich in vitamins A, C, and K, it's more notably one of nature's best chelators, renowned for clearing chemicals and heavy metals (accumulated from the environment) out of the body.

Cinnamon: Cinnamon is a wonder spice. Numerous studies point to its ability to stabilize blood sugar, lower LDL ("bad") cholesterol, fight fungal and bacterial infections, and even protect against cancer.

Cloves: Cloves contain a compound called eugenol, which is an anesthetic and antiseptic. In the Middle Ages, cloves were regularly used to numb toothache pain! They are great for increasing gut secretions, which helps relieve indigestion and constipation.

Coconut (Milk and Oil): The type of fat found in coconut is mostly in the form of medium-chain saturated fatty acids (MCFAs) and, in particular, lauric acid. Unlike saturated fats from animal sources, MCFAs are almost immediately converted into energy by the body, and are unlikely to be stored as fat. Lauric acid is also considered one of nature's most potent superfoods (outside of coconut, breast milk is one of the few places it's found in nature, which proves its importance in human health and development), and is renowned for its antiviral, antibacterial, and antifungal properties.

Coconut Sugar: Coconut sugar is made from evaporating the water out of the sap of the coconut palm. It retains many of the palm's nutrients, and is rich in minerals like iron, zinc, calcium, and potassium. It also contains inulin fiber, which accounts for its low ranking on the glycemic index.

Coffee: Coffee is rich in antioxidants, magnesium, and chromium, and has been found in studies to reduce the risk of type 2 diabetes and Alzheimer's.

Cucumber: Cucumber has the highest water content of any food, and contains an antioxidant called quercetin, found to be anti-inflammatory and bloat reducing.

Curry Powder: While purchased as a single spice, curry powder refers to a blend that varies by region and producer, but typically includes turmeric, coriander, cumin, fenugreek, and chile peppers. Together or alone, these spices are powerful anti-inflammatories and help boost your overall immunity.

Dates: Dates are rich in soluble fiber, which helps keep your blood sugar steady and cleanses your intestines. They're also rich in many minerals, including selenium, manganese, copper, and magnesium, all of which help build strong bones, teeth, and nails.

Fennel: Fennel contains a phytonutrient called anethole, which has been found to reduce inflammation and protect against cancer. It has long been known as a stomach soother, and its high vitamin C levels increase immunity while making skin glow.

Garlic: Garlic is one of the most powerful antiviral and antibacterial foods in existence—studies have found it to be more effective against many bacteria than commonly prescribed antibiotics!

Ginger: Ginger is one of the most powerful anti-inflammatory foods around. It quells nausea and indigestion and helps with arthritis, post-workout pain, and other inflammation-related conditions.

Hazelnuts: Hazelnuts boast the most folate of any tree nut. Folate is famous for helping pregnant moms nurture a healthy fetus, but it has a host of other benefits, including reducing the risk of heart attack and stroke by helping metabolize excess homocysteine in your system. Hazelnuts also contain high quantities of skin- and hair-beautifying manganese and copper.

Honey: Honey has been found to be as effective for cough suppression as over-the-counter remedies. Consuming local honey can even help fight allergies by providing microdoses of local pollen consumed by the bees; when you ingest these tiny amounts of the pollen, your immune system can develop defenses against the allergens without being thrown into overdrive. Honey's antibacterial properties ensure that it's a powerful natural antibiotic, both internally and topically.

Jalapeño: One jalapeño contains 18 percent of your recommended daily dose of vitamin C, and its spiciness can help clear mucus from your nose and throat. Like all hot peppers, jalepeños also contain capsaicin, which has been shown to help with weight loss, especially in the stubborn belly fat area, and offer protection from cancer and heart disease.

Kale: Kale is a cruciferous vegetable in the same family as arugula, Brussels sprouts, and cabbage. All these vegetables contain sulfuric compounds that support your body's detoxification system, helping it eliminate any unwanted toxins. Its dark green color is evidence of high levels of cell-nourishing chlorophyll; plus, it has ample amounts of blood- and bone-aiding vitamin K.

Lavender: Lavender has long been renowned for its ability to soothe both body and mind, and is used as a remedy for anxiety, depression, insomnia, and restlessness, in addition to stomachaches and pains and indigestion.

Lemon: Lemon juice is loaded with vitamin C—one cup contains almost double your daily needs! It helps shift your digestive system into high gear (great if you're ever constipated!), and aids your liver in its own natural detoxification processes. The zest of lemons and other citrus fruit has also been found to be protective against skin cancer.

Lime: The nutrient profile of limes is fairly similar to that of lemons. They contain high amounts of vitamin C, and their acidity matches that of your stomach and gets your digestion going. Lime zest also helps protect against skin cancer.

Mango: Mangoes contain zeaxanthin, an antioxidant that promotes eye health and aids vision. They're also high in vitamins A and C. These are the vitamins to look for in topical skin care (retinol, which is derived from vitamin A, is considered the holy grail of antiaging products). They work similarly inside your body, helping to build the collagen that keeps your skin plump and youthful.

Maple Syrup: Because maple syrup is essentially the sap from the maple tree, all its vitamins and minerals are still intact (unlike processed cane sugar). Just one table-spoon contains one-third of your daily recommended dose of manganese, which helps build healthy skin and bones, and twenty-four free radical-reducing antioxidants. It also has a lower glycemic index than cane sugar, and will help maintain steady blood sugar.

Matcha: Matcha has 137 more antioxidants than regularly brewed green tea (which is already a health superstar in itself!). One of these antioxidants is EGCG, which has been found in numerous studies to have potent cancer-fighting properties.

Mint: The menthol oil found in mint is a much-lauded stomach soother—it's won-derful to cleanse the palate, aid digestion, and fight off nausea. It also helps clear respiratory channels and is a mild natural stimulant, a great way to help wake up without the aid of caffeine. Because of its digestive enzymes and stimulant proper-ties, it can also be an effective weight-loss aid.

Orange: Oranges are vitamin C powerhouses, making your skin glow and helping keep your immune system in top-notch shape. Like lemons and limes, orange zest has been found to be protective against skin cancer.

Peanut Butter: Peanuts, which are not actually nuts but rather legumes, are rich in monounsaturated fatty acids like oleic acid, which help to lower LDL ("bad") cholesterol and increase HDL ("good") cholesterol in the blood. They also pack a protein punch.

Peas: Besides being rich in vitamin K (which reduces your risk of stroke and heart disease), bone-building manganese, filling fiber, and B vitamins (including folate, which is great for pregnant women), peas are one of the few dietary sources of pisumsaponins I and II and pisumosides A and B, phytonutrients that have been found to help combat type 2 diabetes. Studies also indicate that eating a serving or two of peas every day helps reduce the risk of stomach cancer.

Pineapple: Pineapple is the only food source of bromelain, an enzyme that helps you digest and maximize nutrient absorption from your food—it's so potent that it's often sold in supplement form.

Pumpkin: As you might have guessed from their bright orange color, pumpkins are rich in vitamin A—one serving actually contains more than 200 percent of the recommended daily intake. Vitamin A is important for both skin and eye health, and is best consumed with fat (such as coconut milk) to be absorbed properly. Pumpkins are even richer in the heart-healthy electrolyte potassium than bananas, and their fiber will keep you full for hours while also helping to cleanse your intestinal tract. Beta-carotene, an antioxidant abundant in pumpkins, has been found to reduce bodily inflammation and protect against heart disease, lung cancer, and skin cancer.

Raspberries: Raspberries are one of the most fiber-filled fruits, meaning they'll help keep you regular and eliminate bloating. They also contain phytonutrients called raspberry ketones, which increase fat burning and aid liver function. They are highly anti-inflammatory, and have been found to have cancer-preventing properties.

Rose Water: Rose water, made by steam-distilling fresh rose petals, is rich in free radical–annihilating antioxidants and skin-brightening vitamins A and C. It is also a mild relaxant and mood balancer; rose essential oil has been used for centuries for its calming properties—even just sniffing it is effective.

Rosemary: Rosemary is one of the main herbs consumed by residents of certain areas in the Greek islands, where people are among the longest living in the world. Rosemary is powerfully anti-inflammatory, and has been found to reduce both the severity and the frequency of asthma attacks.

Sea Salt: While typical table salt contains only sodium chloride, sea salt and Himalayan salt retain all their nutrients, including potassium, iron, and zinc. Consuming sea salt is a wonderful way to rehydrate yourself and replenish lost electrolytes post-workout.

Spinach: Spinach is rich in vitamin K (one serving contains 1,000 percent of your recommended daily intake) and vitamin A, both of which nourish your cells and skin. As made famous by Popeye, it also contains high amounts of iron, which helps give you energy. Plus, it's packed with fiber, which helps clean out your intestines.

Strawberries: Strawberries boast high quantities of vitamin C, which builds immunity in your body and collagen in your skin. Mashed and mixed with baking soda, they'll even whiten your teeth.

Sweet Potato: The bright orange color of sweet potatoes is a good tip-off that they contain large amounts of vitamin A, a potent antioxidant that boosts your immune system and helps with eye health.

Thyme: Thyme is antiviral and antibacterial, and has been used for centuries to ward off everything from simple coughs to the plague.

Turmeric: Turmeric is prized for its anti-inflammatory benefits—it has been shown in numerous studies to match or even outperform over-the-counter NSAIDs. Turmeric can also be effective in treating diseases like IBS, rheumatoid arthritis, cystic fibrosis, and even cancer.

Watermelon: Watermelons are 91 percent water and, therefore, are super hydrating. That other 9 percent packs a heavy nutrition punch as well—watermelons contain more lycopene, an antioxidant known for ramping up skin protection against the sun, than tomatoes, and an amino acid called L-citrulline that's been found to relieve muscle pain.

Yogurt: Yogurt provides a hefty dose of probiotics, which have been linked to clearer skin, reduced anxiety, better digestion, and weight loss.

Zucchini: Zucchini are packed with collagen- and immunity-boosting vitamin C and bone-building manganese. They're also rich in fiber, which fills you up and helps get your digestive system moving.

ACKNOWLEDGMENTS

There are so many people who have supported me throughout my life, and throughout this book. I feel so lucky to have known each of you.

To Zack, my partner in everything. It feels silly to thank you for this book, so much of it was your doing as much as mine. I would list everything you've done for it and for me but, quite simply, it is everything. You're a husband in a way that surpasses my expectations for the word. I can't imagine this book without you—I can't imagine my life without you—and I'm so thankful to have you by my side. I hope all of the taste testing hasn't ruined pops for you forever.

To my dad, my indefatigable recipe tester, who has believed in me doing great things with my life even when there was absolutely no evidence. To have someone so sure that your life path is the right one, even when you're not, is an amazing gift. Plus, every time you actually made one of my recipes, I got a little zing of excitement.

To my mom, who has always taken such fervent interest in what I'm doing; who always likes all of my photos; who will probably win for "most copies of this cookbook on her shelf." It's so wonderful to have you as my cheerleader.

Susan and Leslie: this book is a direct result of your generosity. *Sprouted Routes* is a direct result of your generosity. You were the best roommates a girl could ask for, the best parents-in-law a wife could dream of, and the best pop testers a chef could hope for. Thank you for always believing in me, and for taste testing Glow Pops before there even *were* Glow Pops.

To Uncle Kev and Aunt Joan, Steve and Aunt Val: you're the closest thing to parents without being parents that exist in my life. I love you bunches, and so appreciate your support over the years.

Thank you, Kim and Jane, for testing so many of these recipes, time and time again. Reader, if you think these pops are delicious, these women are the ones you want to applaud (if you think they're not great, well—we can talk about that some other time). I don't know why you were so gracious with your time, but it's so appreciated.

Alia, my wonderful agent: there would be no Glow Pops without you. From coming up with the best name in history to guiding me through the crazy world of publishing, I couldn't have done this without you—and I'm so glad I didn't have to. You're truly the crème de la crème of agents.

Amanda: you stood out from every other editor I met from the beginning. I hesitate to use the word *spitfire*, but it's truly what you are. You're a fighter, and you're brilliant, and you get me and Glow Pops in a way I'm not sure I even deserve. You're the reason I came to Potter, and I'm so glad I did. Danielle, you've been so wonderful to work with, and I feel so lucky to have you on my team.

To the rest of the team at Potter, Natasha Martin, Carly Gorga, Cathy Hennessy, and Kim Tyner—you guys are all so wonderful. I'm in awe of how beautiful *Glow Pops* is, and it truly has taken a village to take this book from my brain into the hands of people all over the United States. The Potter village is clearly the best one, and I appreciate you all letting me hang out in it for a little while.

To my photo shoot crew: Maeve Sheridan, with her sweet smile and spectacular surfaces; Mariana Velasquez, for making everything look so stunningly beautiful (and artfully messy!), even when working with such tricky subject matter. To the incomparable Lauren Volo, a photographer so much better than I could've even hoped for. These photos are stunning, and it's because of you. I'm honored to have my recipes share these pages with your beautiful images. And to Stephanie Huntwork, the eagle-eyed overseer of it all: your vision so elevated *Glow Pops*, taking it from what could've been a simple little book about ice pops, to a beautiful work of art. Thank you for seeing what it could be, and guiding it to become that.

To my mindbodygreen family, for making our Dumbo office the best place to work (and making my health-nut tendencies seem normal!). To Bella, who helps me write by laying her head on my keyboard. To Bri, for her crazy late night ideas and willingness to talk about pops long after others would be bored. To all of my wonderful family and friends, who never judge my crazy pursuits, and always find the patience to support me and support me, and support me. I'm so lucky to know all of you.

And last but definitely not least—infinite gratitude to all of my wonderful *Sprouted Routes* readers, who send me photos of my recipes, who share their stories, and who keep me going, even when I want to toss my mixing bowl across the room. You let me do what I love, and share what I'm passionate about. Thank you, thank you, thank you to each and every one of you.

INDEX

ABOUT THE AUTHOR

Liz Moody is a writer, recipe developer, and the woman behind *Sprouted Routes,* the healthy recipe and wellness blog. A California native, she spent years traveling the globe as a syndicated newspaper columnist, and has contributed recipes to *Clean Eating, Cooking Light, Goop,* Buzzfeed, mindbodygreen, *Women's Health, Glamour,* and many more. After making homes in San Francisco and London, she's currently based in Brooklyn, where she lives with her cat, Isabella, and husband Zack.

Copyright © 2017 by Liz Moody
Photography copyright © 2017 by Lauren Volo

All rights reserved.
Published in the United States by Clarkson Potter/Publishers, an imprint of the Crown Publishing Group, a division of Penguin Random House LLC, New York.
crownpublishing.com
clarksonpotter.com

CLARKSON POTTER is a trademark and POTTER with colophon is a registered trademark of Penguin Random House LLC.

Library of Congress Cataloging-in-Publication Data

Names: Moody, Liz, author.
Title: Glow pops : super-easy superfood recipes to help you look and feel your best / Liz Moody.
Description: First edition. | New York : Clarkson Potter, [2017]
Identifiers: LCCN 20160311711
ISBN 9780451496447 (hardcover : alk. paper) |
  ISBN 9780451496454 (ebook)
Subjects: LCSH: Ice pops. | LCGFT: Cookbooks.
Classification: LCC TX796.I46 M66 2017 | DDC

641.86/2–dc23 LC record available at https://lccn.loc.gov/2016031171

ISBN 978-0-451-49644-7
Ebook ISBN 978-0-451-49645-4

Design by Stephanie Huntwork
Photography by Lauren Volo
Author Photo by Douglas Gorenstein

10 9 8 7 6 5 4 3 2 1

First Edition

Printed in China